SKI & SNOWBOARD GUIDE TO
WHISTLER BLACKCOMB

by Brian Finestone & Kevin Hodder

Aerial photography courtesy Scott Flavelle. All uncredited photographs by the authors.

Front cover photo of Joe Lammers on Ladies First at Blackcomb by Damian Cromwell.

Distributed by
Gordon Soules Book Publishers Ltd.
1359 Ambleside Lane,
West Vancouver, BC, Canada V7T 2Y9
E-mail: books@gordonsoules.com
Web site: http://www.gordonsoules.com
(604) 922 6588 Fax: (604) 688 5442

Research and text:

Knee Deep Productions
Box 1456 Whistler, B.C. V0N 1B0
www.whistlerguidebooks.com

Layout, design and distribution:

Quickdraw Publications
Box 1786 Squamish, B.C. V8B
Fax: (604) 892-9281
Email: info@quickdrawpublications

D1532777

QUICKDRAW PUBLICATIONS

KNEE DEEP KDP PRODUCTIONS

Title page photo: Damian Cromwell, Back cover photos: Damian Cromwell (right) and Bryn Hughes (left)

Table of Contents

contents photo: Bryn Hughes

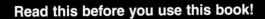

Disclaimer

Read this before you use this book!

Warning: Skiing and snowboarding are sports which involve inherent risks. Participating in these sports may result in injury or death.

This guidebook is intended to be used by **expert** skiers and snowboarders only. The terrain described within is dangerous and requires a high level of experience to negotiate.

This guidebook is a compilation of information from several sources. As a result the authors cannot confirm the accuracy of any specific detail. Difficulty ratings are subjective and may vary depending on your own personal experience and the conditions on the mountain. There may be misinformation in regards to run description, condition, or difficulty.

This guidebook does not give the user the right to access any terrain described within. The Ski Patrol may limit access to any part of the mountain at any time. It is your responsibility to adhere to all closures.

Introduction

The inspiration for this book came from the recognition that Whistler and Blackcomb are blessed with over 7,000 skiable acres, four glaciers, over 20 alpine bowls and 33 lifts. These are two huge mountains and finding your way around can be very confusing (even with careful consultation of the trail map). Without someone showing you around it can take the better part of a season just to figure out what your favorite runs are and how to access them. In short, anyone coming for a week-long vacation has to learn pretty fast! This book is an attempt to

Blackcomb

remedy this issue by presenting detailed information of the ski area in a user-friendly format.

As dedicated rock-climbers, the authors have used guidebooks that would allow them to show up at a distant climbing area and enjoy the best routes almost immediately. The intention of this book is to bring a format long used by authors of climbing guidebooks to the ski area.

Over 7,000 acres of skiable terrain!

Whistler

How To Use This Book

Congratulations! You have purchased the ultimate reference for skiers and snowboarders wishing to maximize their experience at Whistler Blackcomb. Each chapter within this book gives an overview of the terrain that is accessed by a specific chairlift. Run and access information is presented in a number of ways including aerial photographs, symbols and text. The aerial photographs are superimposed with labels and markings and become an excellent tool for choosing what area you want to explore next. The symbols are used to provide a significant amount of information at a glance.

Sample Run Photo

PERMANENTLY CLOSED AREA

BOUNDARY LINE OF PERMANENTLY CLOSED AREA

95 RUN NUMBER

LINE OF TRAVERSE (MAY ALSO INDICATE A BOOTPACK)

LINE OF RUN

NAME OF RUN

SKI AREA BOUNDARY LINE

Please refer to the key below to familiarize yourself with the symbol definitions. The written text is intended to provide any further information that cannot be directly presented through photograph or symbol.

This book is designed to be used in conjunction with the mountain trail map. Trail maps are available free of charge throughout the resort and for viewing at www.whistlerblackcomb.com/maps/. Keep both the map and this book handy while riding on the mountain. Both are pocket size for a reason!

Symbols

● Novice terrain	🌲 Treed area	Rocky - requires <u>lots</u> of snow to be skiable
■ Intermediate	N	Avalanche debris hazard
◆ Advanced	E	Traverse tracks hazard
◆◆ Expert	S	Direction the slope faces
◆◆◆ Super expert	W	Cut-bank hazard
❶ Average run		Falling in a crevasse hazard
❷ Good run	Must-hike-up-to access	Gondola
❸ Excellent run	Jump-in access	T-Bar
POW Powder common on this slope	Often crowded	Triple chairlift
Moguls common on this slope	Scary, exposed run	Quad chairlift
▨ Groomed	A fall <i>will</i> result in injury	HP Half-pipe
Great cruising run	Falling off a cliff hazard	T Terrain park
	Cornice collapse hazard	The tick box

Furthering Your Enjoyment of Whistler Blackcomb

As dedicated powder hounds are prone to do, we suggest calling the "Snow Report" (see page 19) before heading up the hill. Calling the report will answer the following questions:

☐ Is there any new snow?

☐ Is avalanche control being conducted?

☐ What is the current weather and forecast?

☐ What runs have been groomed?

☐ Are there any special events?

Gaining this information will allow you to better plan your day. If avalanche control is being conducted, there will likely be a delay in opening the upper mountain. Once you arrive, refer to the "lightboards" that are placed around the mountain. The lightboards will tell you what lifts are open, how long the lines are at each lift and what lifts are on standby. As you know, on powder days, timing is everything. You will want to anticipate which lifts are opening next in order to get your share of fresh snow. Here is the typical (yet certainly not guaranteed) order of lift openings after avalanche clearance.

Whistler: Roundhouse Zone ⇒ T-Bars ⇒ Harmony Express Chair ⇒ Peak Chair.

Blackcomb: Wizard/Solar Coaster Express Chair ⇒ Jersey Cream Express Chair ⇒ Crystal Chair ⇒ Seventh Heaven Express Chair ⇒ Glacier Express Chair ⇒ Showcase T-Bar.

Always remember, the opening and closing of all runs is done at the discretion of the Ski Patrol. It is your responsibility to determine whether the runs described in this book are open or closed before skiing or riding the run.

Photographer Damian Cromwell enjoys the
other side of the lense. Photo: Bryn Hughes

Trail Designations ⬤ ☐ ◆ ⧫ ⧫⧫

All ski runs are not created equal! Many people find the Blue runs at Whistler to be as hard as the Black Diamond runs at other ski areas. So, how do they classify the runs at Whistler Blackcomb? Trails are given a difficulty rating based on an evaluation of the slope's width, average gradient, and the steepest 30 meters of pitch. A simple rating of Green, Blue or Black Diamond does not do the variety of terrain at Whistler Blackcomb justice, therefore, we have added Double Black Diamond and Triple Black Diamond to this guide. Remember, with the increase in difficulty comes an increase in the risk of longer and more hazardous falls!

Signs

The following is the interpretation of some of the signs at Whistler Blackcomb and a look at the consequences of skiing beyond them.

Ski Area Boundary
This sign indicates the border of Whistler Blackcomb's patrolled area. Skiing or riding outside the area is done at your own risk. It is your responsibility to have the adequate knowledge to travel safely in avalanche terrain and to carry the essential personal-safety gear.

People who require rescue from the backcountry can and will be charged for their rescue.

In early season, Ski Area Boundary signs often exist within the ski area. These boundaries denote parts of the hill that are not yet ready to open. As a result, there are no hazard markings, no ski patrol and no sweep of these areas at the end of the day.

Permanently Closed

These signs indicate areas of the mountain that are NEVER open. These are areas within the ski area that are determined to be unsuitable for skiing. The danger of entering these areas often extends beyond the risk to the offending skier or rider, because their actions threaten skiers on runs below. Passes will be revoked from anyone who disobeys these signs.

Closed / Avalanche Hazard

These signs are used to temporarily close areas within the ski area. Avalanche closures keep guests out of harm's way during active avalanche control (explosives!) or when the hazard grows too high and control is not possible. Passes will be revoked from anyone who disobeys these signs.

Closed

Runs are closed for a variety of reasons. These reasons may include: thin snow cover, ditches or holes, fallen trees, races or other events are taking place, snow making or other machinery is operating, etc. Passes will be revoked from anyone who disobeys these signs.

Code of Conduct

In recent years, the alpine areas of Whistler Blackcomb have seen a rise in the aggressive attitude of skiers during powder days. Think of this as a mild form of what surfers call "localism". If we all adhere to a certain set of ethics then cooler heads will prevail and everyone will enjoy the day. Remember, we're all there for the same thing!

- ☐ **Poaching**: Skiing or riding in areas designated as Permanent Closures or Avalanche Closures during avalanche-control operations affects everyone. The Ski Patrol's "Blaster-in-Charge" must stop all explosives-control efforts until the area has been swept and confirmed clear. In the past, this has delayed the opening of alpine areas for hours!

- ☐ **Lift Lines:** Everyone will get to the top eventually. Don't push, shove, butt in, or let your friends in. Besides, everyone knows, "Friends don't have friends on powder days."

- ☐ **T-Bars**: If you cannot ride a T-bar, a 20-centimetre powder day is not the day to learn, unless you are willing to suffer the wrath of the powder hounds!

- ☐ **Bootpacks**: A "bootpack" is a place where people walk up slopes to access certain areas. These areas can become quite congested during powder days. If you become too tired to keep walking up the bootpack, step off to the side while you rest and let the people behind you pass!

- ☐ **Powder Preservation**: Because of the typical post-snowfall feeding frenzy, we all need to do our part. Put your line down tight beside your buddie's.

- ☐ **Sideslipping:** Entrance ways into some chutes become a horrendous groove when this activity goes unchecked. If you can't ride in, maybe you shouldn't be there.

- ☐ **Garbage**: Pack it out! No one wants to see trash on the mountains.

- □ **Smoking**: If you smoke, pack out your butts. Respect others in the lift line and on the chair; ask before you light up.

- □ **Lock- It Up**: Many skis, and especially snowboards, are ripped off every year. Lock up your gear, check it at the Store-A-Ski, or stash it! Send these losers somewhere else to steal things!

- □ **Peeing:** Use the toilets located at the restaurants. If you can't wait, find a boulder or tree, but don't leave your name written in yellow snow.

BE AWARE

SKI AND RIDE WITH CARE

Know the Alpine Responsibility Code. You will be held accountable to it! In addition to this, please...

◇ Don't ski or ride alone!

◇ Know where you are at all times! If in doubt, ask. Each year, many passes are revoked and many injuries occur because people unwittingly enter closed runs or terrain beyond their abilities.

◇ Respect the folks skiing the lower mountain; you were there once, too!

◇ Wear a helmet...it could save your life!

"You fall, we haul" - Patrol Motto.

15

Avalanche Control At Whistler Blackcomb

The avalanche control program is designed to reduce the hazard within the ski area by intentionally starting avalanches before the skiing public is present. The individual in charge of directing the program is the Avalanche Forecaster. The Forecaster will begin by assessing the snow stability and avalanche hazard through a detailed analysis of several factors including snowfall amounts, temperature, winds, humidity and weather forecasts. The Forecaster will then direct a crew of Ski Patrollers to control the hazard in an efficient manner so that the terrain is open as soon as possible. This crew will leave the valley

Cornice blast!

before dawn and will be skiing before the majority of us have had our second cup of coffee.

Most avalanche control involves the use of explosives to initiate the activity. It is not uncommon for 200kg of explosives to be used on the mountains during a morning when the avalanche hazard is high.

The patrollers, working in teams of two, are assigned specific "routes" which they are responsible for controlling. They will deposit their explosives on the slopes using several methods of deployment. The primary method is called a "hand charge". A hand charge is simply a stick of explosive with a fuse and igniter cap. The

Bomb preparation.

teams literally ski or hike along the ridge tops with a pack full of explosives. When they arrive at the point above a predetermined target, they will pull a hand charge out of their pack, light the fuse and throw the bomb onto the slope or cornice. Once the fuse is lit the team has 90 seconds to get to a safe spot, plug their ears and wait.

Walk softly!

If the terrain is too difficult (or dangerous) to access on skis, then an aerial "bomb-tram" may be utilized. A bomb-tram is a permanent structure that is installed across a span of terrain and works like a giant clothesline. After explosives are attached to the line and the fuse is lit, the Patroller can "wheel" the assembly out over the desired place on the slope. Bomb-trams are installed in the alpine areas of both mountains. The most visible tram is off to your left as you ride the Peak Chair past tower 10.

"Avalaunchers" are permanently installed guns that are used to shoot explosive projectiles at otherwise inaccessible pieces of terrain. An avalauncher is operated by releasing a measured amount

Bomb-tram on Blackcomb.

of pressurized nitrogen gas through a barrel thus propelling a projectile toward a target like a giant peashooter. This peashooter, however, can lob a one-kilogram rocket over a distance of 2000m! There are currently 7 avalaunchers installed at Whistler Blackcomb. **17**

Avalanche Control At Whistler Blackcomb

When the weather permits, the most effective and time-efficient method of delivering explosives to the slopes is by dropping them out of a helicopter. "Helibombing" involves three patrollers in the helicopter: the Bombardier, the Explosives Prep and the Recorder. A fourth patroller remains on the ground assembling the explosives for each round.

The most utilized non-explosive method of avalanche control is "ski-cutting". This method involves skiing across the start zones of avalanche paths to initiate activity. This can be a very dangerous technique and is most often used by the Patrol to remove small "pocket' avalanches that were not initiated by earlier explosive control.

It is easy to perceive avalanche control as a "dream job" however it can be a harrowing experience, especially for the first timer. Imagine an hour within a helicopter, hovering close to the ground with the door open and the smoke of burning fuses filling the cabin. Add a little turbulence from winds and you have the perfect recipe for motion sickness! The next morning you may be expected to ski double-black diamond terrain with a pack full of bombs. Needless to say falling is not an option!

The Avalanche Control Program is performed by a dedicated group of professionals with the mandate of opening the terrain as soon as possible. Please respect them for working hard behind the scenes and allowing us to access the goods!

Heli-bomb Crew

Useful Phone Numbers

WHISTLER BLACKCOMB SNOW PHONE
   (604) 932 4211- WHISTLER
   (604) 687 7507- VANCOUVER
BLACKCOMB PATROL SNOW REPORT
   (604) 935 5596
ON-MOUNTAIN EMERGENCY
   (604) 935 5555
AFTER-HOURS EMERGENCY
   (604) 905 5484 - MISSING PERSONS

Website

This site contains excellent information on weather, snow conditions, avalanche hazard, road conditions, events, live web cams, etc.

   www.whistlerblackcomb.com

Operating Hours

DATE	OPENING	CLOSING
NOV - JAN 28	8:30 AM	3:00 PM
JAN 29 - FEB 27	8:30 AM	3:30 PM
FEB 28 - APR 17	8:30 AM	4:00 PM
APR 18 - JUN 5	9:00 AM	4:00 PM

Hazards

Tree Wells: More people are killed in coastal snow regions by tree wells than by avalanches!

A tree well is a phenomenon unique to big mountains with deep snow packs. A tree well forms when snow falling on evergreens accumulates between the trees but not around the tree trunk. As the snow is shed from the branches above it falls away from the tree creating a moat around the base of the trunk. As the snow gets deeper so does the tree well.

The danger exists when a person falls over in the snow and ends up with their body upside down in the tree well. As the person struggles to get out, the hole fills with snow, potentially burying the victim. People have died of suffocation in the wells of both large trees and small saplings. Unlike avalanches, tree wells cannot be reasonably controlled and the hazard exists anywhere on the mountain once the snow pack exceeds one meter (about 3.5 feet) in depth. When riding in the trees it is very important to maintain audible contact with everyone in your party. It is recommended that avid tree skiers have a whistle on their jackets for this purpose.

Dropping the knee in the trees.

Cornices: These are formed when wind-transported snow is deposited on the lee aspect of a ridge. The dense snow forms meringue-like tongues that overhang the slopes below. Although the snow appears capable of supporting a skier's weight, it can fracture and drop the rider (and massive amounts of snow) over the edge and down the slope.

Entry into slopes guarded by cornices is tricky and dangerous business. Many of the runs described in this book involve negotiating an entry around a cornice. Whistler Blackcomb's avalanche control program includes the "trimming" of cornices with explosives. This preventative measure ensures that the cornices don't grow too big, but does not guarantee that they are safe to walk on or won't fall naturally with changing temperatures.

All cornices should be treated with respect and considered time bombs ready to collapse. The best way to gain access to the slope below a cornice is to stay well back from the edge and scout for any obvious entry that cuts in at a natural notch. If no such entrance exists, it may be best to leave that line for another day.

Entry guarded by a cornice.

Weather

In the Coast Range of British Columbia there are three main weather patterns. Each of them affect the snow conditions. Thankfully, the most common pattern is the southwest flow, which brings moderate temperatures and predictable snow to the mountains. The second is the dreaded Pineapple Express, which brings very moist, warm air up from the subtropics. High freezing levels and rain are associated with a Pineapple Express.

The final pattern is the high-pressure northerly outflow, in which cold air from the arctic flows south and leaves the mountain in a period of drought. Very cold temperatures are likely in the alpine.

Daylight Hours (Valley)

Month	Monthly Average
November	9:52
December	8:29
January	8:17
February	9:25
March	11:00
April	12:53
May	14:36
June	15:57
July	16:10
August	15:08
September	13:28
October	11:40

photo: Tim Smith

Sometimes you have to make your own weather. Snowmaking on Blackcomb (foreground) and Whistler (across the valley).

Snowfall Averages*

November	88cm	35"
December	284cm	112"
January	183cm	72"
February	109cm	43"
March	198cm	78"
April	118cm	46"
May	53cm	21"

*Measurements taken at 1600m/5249'.

Valley Temperature Averages

Month	High (c)	Low (c)	High (f)	Low (f)
November	+5	-1	+41	+30
December	-1	-5	+30	+23
January	-2	-8	+28	+18
February	+3	-5	+37	+23
March	+8	-3	+46	+27
April	+11	-2	+52	+36
May	+17	+7	+62	+44
June	+21	+9	+70	+48
July	+27	+11	+80	+52
August	+27	+11	+80	+52
September	+20	+8	+65	+46
October	+16	+3	+60	+38

Alpine Temperature Averages

Month	High (c)	Low (c)	High (f)	Low (f)
December	-5	-12	+23	+10
January	-5	-12	+23	+10
February	-5	-12	+23	+10
March	+5	-8	+41	+18
April	+5	-8	+41	+18
May	+5	-8	+41	+18

Here's a good rule of thumb about what air temperature in Vancouver relates to snowfall in Whistler. Typically, if the temperature in Vancouver is 7 degrees Celsius or colder, and it is raining, we will see snow in Whistler Village. If the temperature is 10 degrees in Vancouver, there will be freezing temperatures at the top of the Wizard Chair on Blackcomb.

Check the temperature and precipitation charts in order to get a feel for what you can expect while you are here.

WHISTLER

BOOMER
BOWL

HARMONY
RIDGE

HARMONY
BOWL

ROUNDHOUSE
LODGE

VILLAGE BASE AREA

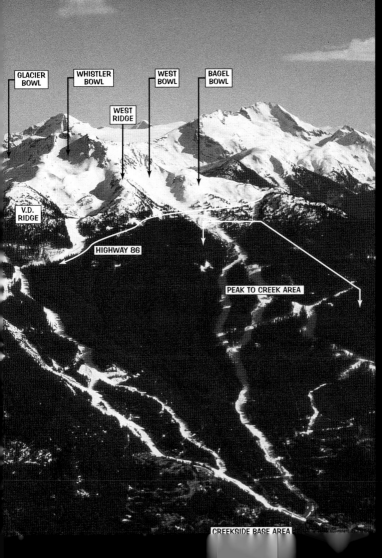

GLACIER BOWL

WHISTLER BOWL

WEST BOWL

BAGEL BOWL

WEST RIDGE

V.D. RIDGE

HIGHWAY 86

PEAK TO CREEK AREA

CREEKSIDE BASE AREA

WHISTLER

Whistler - Vertical Chart

	Village	Olympic	Ravan's Nest	Whistler Creek	Little Whistler
Village	0	1157'	2051'	n/a	4725'
Olympic	1157'	0	919'	n/a	3593'
Ravan's Nest	2051'	919'	0	2113'	2674'
Whistler Creek	n/a	n/a	2113'	0	4799'
Little Whistler	4725'	3593'	2674'	4799'	0
Chickpea	3239'	2107'	1188'	3313'	1486'
Roundhouse	3855'	2723'	1804'	3929'	870'
Peak	4946'	3814'	2895'	5020'	221'

Chickpea	Roundhouse	Peak
3239'	3855'	4946'
2107'	2723'	3814'
1188'	1804'	2895'
3313'	3929'	5020'
1486'	870'	221'
0	616'	1707'
616'	0	1091
1707'	1091'	0

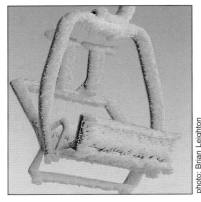

photo: Brian Leighton

photo: Alain Denis

Whistler images clockwise from far left: skiing with views of the Black Tusk, the Roundhouse Lodge, rimed chair, powder cruising and an alpine overview.

Roundhouse Zone West

The Roundhouse Lodge is located at the top of the Village Gondola and adjacent to the top of both the Emerald Express and the Big Red Express chairs. The zone below the lodge, although dominated by intermediate and novice terrain, does contain some interesting runs.

The beauty of the Roundhouse Zone is that it remains open in extremely inclement weather, which, let's face it, Whistler has its share of. If the T-Bars, Harmony Express and Peak Chair are closed due to weather, these runs may be the best option.

1. Franz's Meadow . . . .
A beautiful open bowl; deservedly popular. From the Roundhouse, head down Pony Trail

(Green) until it flattens out under the Big Red Express. From here, keep your elevation and traverse over to the meadow.

2. Lower V.D. Chutes (via the Goat Path) . . . . .

Caution - There are a lot of *ugly* cliffs in the area below the Goat Path. Go with someone who knows the area until you have it figured out for yourself! The Goat Path can also be taken all the way over to the last pitch of Grande Finale, however, it provides a short run after a long traverse.

3. C.C. . . . .

Start from behind the top of the Whistler Village Gondola.

4. Paleface . . . .

As for C.C.

Paleface

ROUNDHOUSE LODGE

TOP OF WHISTLER VILLAGE GONDOLA

PALEFACE

C.C.

BIG RED EXPRESS CHAIR

PONY TRAIL

Roundhouse Zone East

Access these runs by beginning down G.S. and breaking left when the signs indicate.

5. Ratfink . . . .
Some interesting steep rolls and cliffs.

6. Chunky's Choice . . . .
Considered a classic when bump skiing was the rage! Dust off that "daffy" with which you used to impress the chicks. Scott boots, Spalding skis and Schneider stretch pants required!

7. Dapper's Delight . . . .
The former Blue Chair lift line. A fall line shot with a good pitch.

8. Seppo's (no photo) . . . .
The former Black Chair lift line. A ridiculously off-fall line run, but great during a storm. The run is best accessed by the Garbonzo Express chair. Look for the signs.

ROUNDHOUSE LODGE

WHISTLER MOUNTAIN
NINTENDO HALF-PIPE

EMERALD EXPRESS
CHAIR

G.S.

6

5

RAT FINK

7

G.S.

DAPPER'S
DELIGHT

CHUNKY'S CHOICE

BOTTOM OF
HARMONY EXPRESS CHAIR

31

Victoria Jealouse holds on for the ride. Photo: Bryn Hughes

Dan Treadway frozen in space on Ladies First. Photo: Damian Cromwell

The T-Bars

The only two T-Bars on Whistler Mountain run parallel to one another and can be easily accessed from the Roundhouse Lodge via a well-marked cat track. The T-Bars are often the first <u>alpine</u> lifts to open after a storm. All runs listed in the T-Bar section can be accessed by either the Harmony Express or the Peak Chair, however, they are listed here because the T-Bars are the lowest lifts allowing access.

Headwall Zone

9. T-Bar Bowl . . . .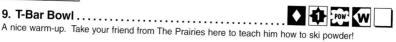

A nice warm-up. Take your friend from The Prairies here to teach him how to ski powder!

10. Headwall . . . .

Great terrain beside the T-Bar. This is a good run to do a couple of times while awaiting the imminent Peak Chair opening! Access by a short hike from the start of the traverse to Ridge Run.

11. Staggerhome Chute . . . .

A very narrow chute accessed via Ridge Run.

12. G.S. Start . . . .

. . . .

A short slope above Pika's Traverse.

13. Jump Hill . . . .

. . . .

This steep slope is above the shack where the Whistler Ski Patrol prepares bombs for avalanche control.

14. Ridge Run . . . .

. . . .

Sometimes groomed allowing for hero turns down to the Roundhouse level.

Lower Harmony Zone

15. Montana's Mistake . . . .

. . . .

Varied terrain off the top of the T-Bar.

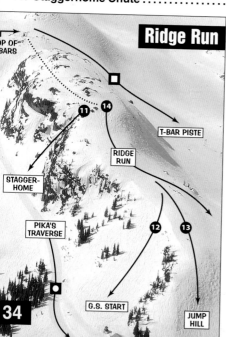

16. Die Hard . . .

Short steep pitch next to the Harmony Waterfall. Bruce Willis would be proud! Photo on page 37.

17. Boomer Bowl. . . . .

. . . .

A wide concave bowl. Definitely worth the traverse from the T-Bars. See photos on pages 36 & 43.

18. Wet Dreams

Small, scrappy trees strewn across a nice slope. See photos on pages 36 & 43.

19. Gun Barrels

Steep, tight chutes through the trees. Get there before the crowds! Access these lines by resisting the temptation to drop into Boomer Bowl. Traverse high towards Harmony Ridge until you are looking down the barrel! See photos on pages 36 and 43.

20. Waterface...

A nice little slope that gets tracked quickly since it is right next to the lift. Photo on page 37.

21. Bitter End. .

Similar to Waterface. Photo on page 37.

22. Boot Chutes

Great little lines down to the base of the Harmony Express chair. Photos on pages 36 and 43.

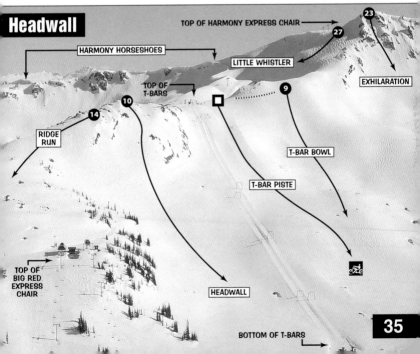

Headwall

TOP OF HARMONY EXPRESS CHAIR

HARMONY HORSESHOES

LITTLE WHISTLER

EXHILARATION

TOP OF T-BARS

23

27

9

14

10

RIDGE RUN

T-BAR BOWL

T-BAR PISTE

TOP OF BIG RED EXPRESS CHAIR

HEADWALL

BOTTOM OF T-BARS

TOP OF HARMONY
EXPRESS CHAIR

HARMONY HORSESHOES

29

HARMONY RIDGE

UPPER
McCONKEY'S

CAMEL BACKS

HARMONY PISTE

TRAVERSE TO BOOMER
BOWL FROM TOP OF T-BARS

17

BOOMER BOWL

19

WET DREAMS

18

LOWER
McCONKEY'S

22

BOOT
CHUTES

GUN BARRELS

36

TOP OF
PEAK CHAIR

WHISTLER BOWL

GLACIER BOWL

27

TOP OF
T-BARS

16

15

HARMONY WATERFALL

20

21

DIE HARD

MONTANA'S
MISTAKE

WATER FACE

BITTER END

6

CHUNKY'S CHOICE

7

DAPPER'S
DELIGHT

G.S.

37

Harmony Express Chair - Little Whistler

Access Exhilaration, Excitation, Glacier Wall and Dilemma by hiking to the top of the ridge which is to your right as you get off the chair. There is often a well-worn bootpack.

23. Exhilaration. . . . .

Very steep and narrow. Can take several humid storms before it has adequate snow cover. Additional photos on pages 35 and 56.

24. Excitation. . . . .

The best of the bunch. A steep, tight line designated by a rock pillar two-thirds of the way down on the left. Mega! Additional photo on page 56.

25. Glacier Wall . . . .

Wait for adequate coverage before you put your balls to this wall! Additional photo page 56.

26. Dilemma. . . . .

A steep, interesting line. Additional photo on page 56.

27. Little Whistler. . . . .

Nice long run underneath the upper lift line. Additional photos on pages 35, 37 and 56.

28. Camel Backs. . . . .

The large mounds at the base of Little Whistler.

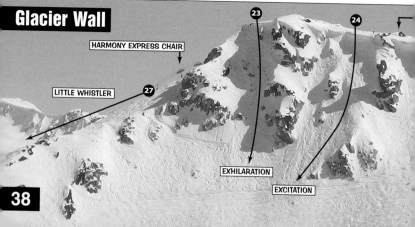

Glacier Wall

HARMONY EXPRESS CHAIR

LITTLE WHISTLER

EXHILARATION

EXCITATION

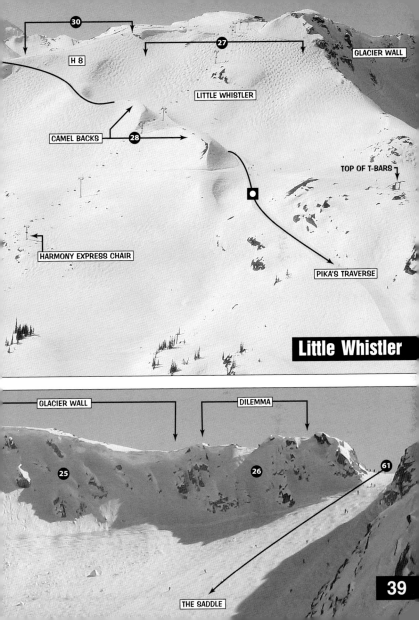

30

H 8

27

GLACIER WALL

LITTLE WHISTLER

CAMEL BACKS **28**

TOP OF T-BARS

HARMONY EXPRESS CHAIR

PIKA'S TRAVERSE

Little Whistler

GLACIER WALL

DILEMMA

25

26

61

THE SADDLE

39

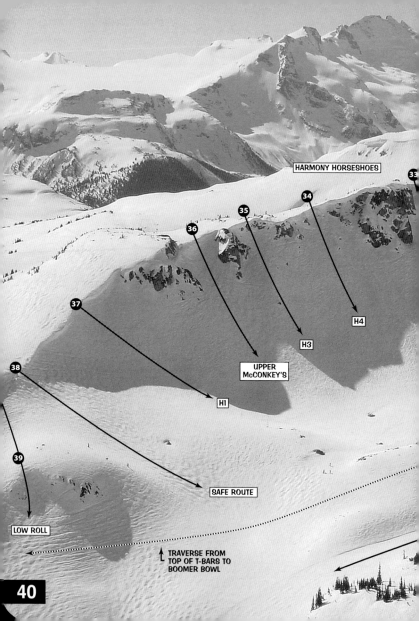

HARMONY HORSESHOES

33

34

35

36

37

38

39

H4

H3

UPPER
McCONKEY'S

H1

SAFE ROUTE

LOW ROLL

TRAVERSE FROM
TOP OF T-BARS TO
BOOMER BOWL

40

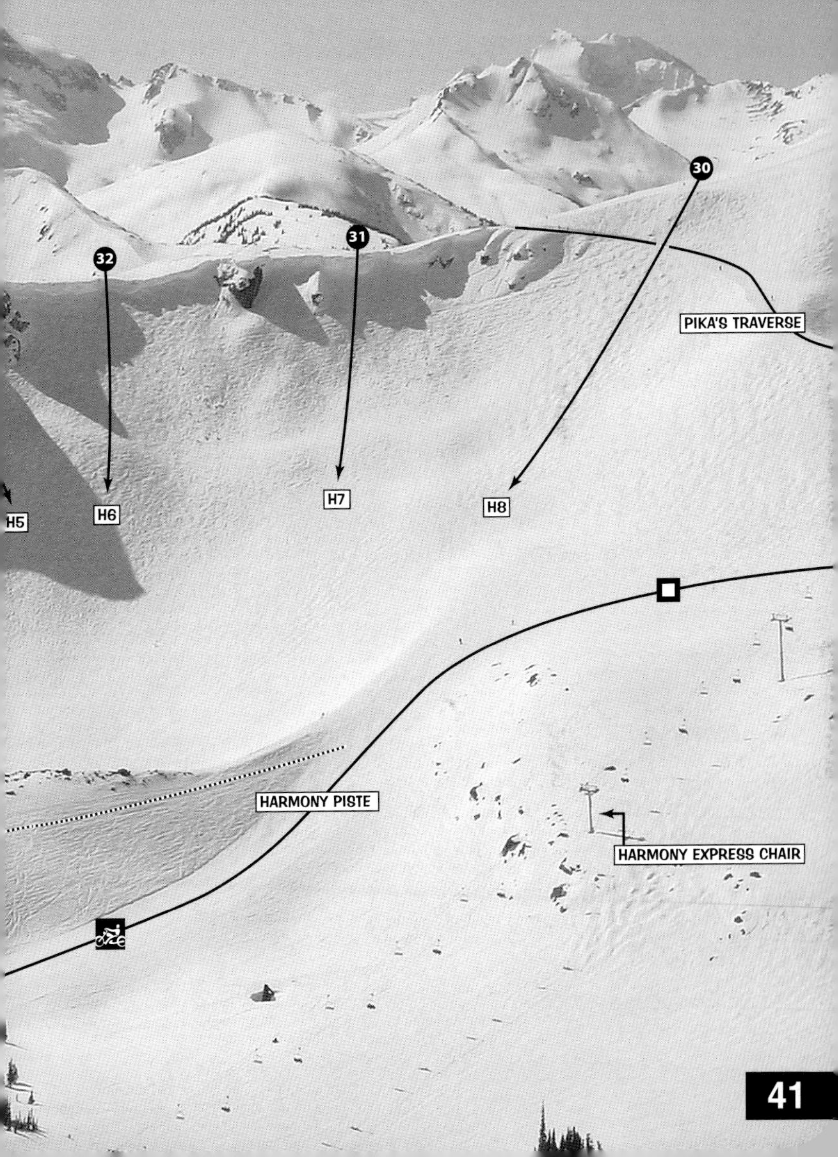

32

31

30

PIKA'S TRAVERSE

H5

H6

H7

H8

HARMONY PISTE

HARMONY EXPRESS CHAIR

Harmony Express Chair - Harmony Ridge

This corniced ridge has several short chutes. All are accessed from Harmony Ridge.

29. Harmony Ridge. . . . .
Consider this run your artery to some of the best terrain the Harmony Chair has to offer. Remember, you're sharing this run with skiers of all abilities. Additional photo on page 36.

30. Horseshoe 8. . . . .

31. Horseshoe 7. . . . .

32. Horseshoe 6. . . . .

33. Horseshoe 5. . . . .
The tightest and scariest of the Horseshoes.

34. Horseshoe 4. . . . .

35. Horseshoe 3. . . . .

36. Upper McConkey's. . . . .
Named after Whistler's father of steep skiing, "Diamond" Jim McConkey.

37. Horseshoe 1. . . . .

38. Safe Route. . . . .
The first lower angle slope leading off Harmony Ridge (Blue) to Harmony Bowl. Connects nicely with the traverse to Boomer Bowl or Lower McConkey's.

39. Low Roll. . . . .
A good line. Can be used to access Boomer Bowl and Wet Dreams.

40. KC Roll. . . . .
A very steep slope.

41. Kaleidoscope. . . . .
As above, only better!

Boomer Bowl

HARMONY HORSESHOES

HARMONY RIDGE

LOW ROLL

KC ROLL

KALEIDOSCOPE

TRAVERSE FROM TOP OF T-BARS TO BOOMER BOWL

BOOMER BOWL

HARMONY PISTE

LOWER McCONKEY'S

WET DREAMS

GUN BARRELS

BOOT CHUTES

HARMONY RIDGE

43

TOP OF PEAK CHAIR

TOP OF HARMONY
EXPRESS CHAIR

42

29

SUN BOWL

44

CRESCENDO

HIDDEN CHUTE

BURNT STEW TRAIL

44

HARMONY RIDGE

29

HARVEY'S HARROW

45

ROBERTSON'S RUN

46

══════ ## Harmony Express Chair - Sun Bowl

The runs in this zone face predominantly east, which can be either a curse or a blessing. It can be the first zone to soften up after a cold spring night or it can be the first to have dry, new snow ruined by powerful solar rays. Access Sun Bowl by heading left off the top of the Harmony Express chair. Almost immediately, you will see signs directing you (skier's right) to Sun Bowl.

42. Sun Bowl. . . . . ◆ ❷ ❀ Ⓔ ☐

Great terrain and lots of it. Be sure to wear your shades!

Sun Bowl

BURNT STEW TRAIL

42 29 HARMONY RIDGE

SUN BOWL

43

SUN BOWL CHUTES

CRESCENDO

43. Sun Bowl Chutes . . . . ◆◆ **2** POW E 🏔 ☐

44. Hidden Chute . . . . ◆ **1** POW 🌲 E 🎿 🚡 ☐
A scrappy, off-fallline diagonal run.

45. Harvey's Harrow . . . . ◆ **3** POW 🌲 E 🚡 ☐
A classic gladed slope with a consistent pitch.

46. Robertson's Run . . . . ◆ **3** POW 🌲 E 🚡 ☐
Great skiing through glades and well-spaced old-growth trees.

Hidden Chute

47

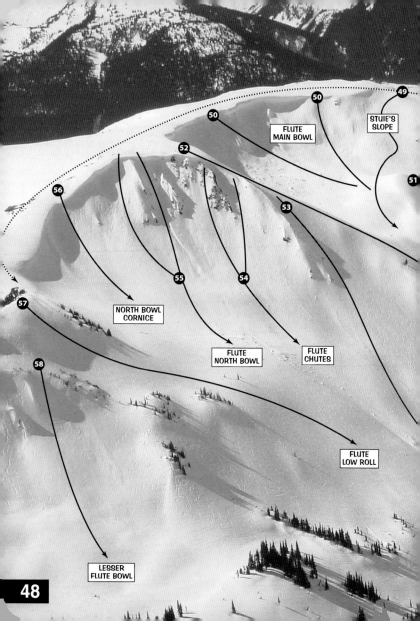

STUIE'S SLOPE

FLUTE MAIN BOWL

NORTH BOWL CORNICE

FLUTE NORTH BOWL

FLUTE CHUTES

FLUTE LOW ROLL

LESSER FLUTE BOWL

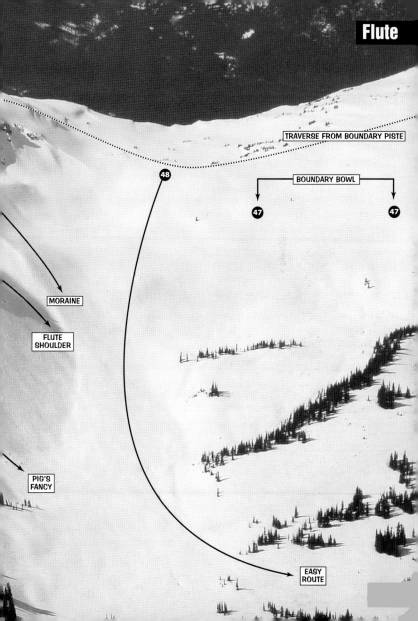

Flute

TRAVERSE FROM BOUNDARY PISTE

BOUNDARY BOWL

47

47

48

MORAINE

FLUTE
SHOULDER

PIG'S
FANCY

EASY
ROUTE

═══════════════════ **Harmony Express Chair - Flute**

Flute sits on the border to Garibaldi Provincial Park, forming the highest point of the "Musical Bumps" ridge. A new experience for skiers and riders at Whistler Blackcomb, this area is open to visitors willing to walk up and "earn their turns". The area will receive avalanche control and Ski Patrol attention, but grooming will be limited to a track into the top and a rescue road out from the bottom.

From the top of Harmony Express Chair, take the Burnt Stew trail (Green) to its junction with Boundary Piste (Blue). Continue along Boundary Piste to Boundary Bowl. From the top of Boundary Bowl, traverse to the base of the west ridge of Flute. Shoulder your gear and start hiking up the established bootpack from here! The unofficial record for trips up Flute in one day is 8!

47. Boundary Bowl. . . . .
When the visibility is poor in the high alpine, don't forget about Boundary Bowl. There are just enough trees flanking the bowl to provide reference in flat light.

48. Easy Route . . . .
The easy route requires little or no hiking and descends the open meadow into the Flute basin. A great first run on Flute that allows you to get a feel for the terrain.

49. Stuie's Slope. . . . .
A steep face leading into the main bowl. Stuie's Run is named for a Whistler local who was killed in an avalanche on this slope. Sadly, this is one of the few ways to have a run named after you.

50. Flute Main Bowl. . . . .
The main bowl, although good, is often littered with avalanche debris. Watch out!

51. Moraine. . . . .
The Moraine is another line that does not involve the full hike to the top.

52. Flute Shoulder. . . . .
The shoulder is probably the best bang for your buck; it is the longest ski run at a consistent grade in the Flute Area. Don't miss it!

53. Pig's Fancy. . . . .
Although not the steepest run in the zone, this gem catches the best powder of any line on Flute. Find your way onto the shoulder and break off skier's right onto the steeper slope. If you get there first don't stop until you get to the bottom, it could be the run of your life!

54. Flute Chutes. . . . .
These steep chutes can be tricky to get into. The reward is a handful of steep jump turns into sweet bowl cruising below.

55. Flute North Bowl. . . . .
The entire North bowl offers great powder skiing and is usually last to get shredded because of the long hike up.

56. North Bowl Cornice. . . . .
The cornice at this end of the bowl forms a natural ramp, which gains access to great riding on the right side of the bowl.

57. Flute Low Roll. . . . .
Lower angled skiing through a series of tree islands, reminiscent of a classic heli-ski run.

58. Lesser Flute Bowl. . . . .
Lesser Flute is a smaller bowl on the east end of the series of bowls that offers great lines. The walk is a little longer but for those seeking to get away from the crowds you won't be disappointed.

Dan Treadway lost in a wave of snow in Whistler's Sunbowl.   Photo: Damian Cromwell

Victoria Jealouse leans into a beautiful powder turn. Photo: Bryn Hughes

TOP OF HARMONY CHAIR

LITTLE WHISTLER

GLACIER BOWL

TOP OF PEAK CHAIR

WHISTLER BOWL

WEST RIDGE

61

72

ROUNDHOUSE LODGE

EMERALD EXPRESS CHAIR

TOP OF PEAK CHAIR

GLACIER BOWL

WHISTLER BOWL

60

59

70

61

54

GLACIER BOWL

GLACIER WALL

TOP OF PEAK CHAIR

WHISTLER BOWL

Permanently Closed Area

WEST BOWL

WEST RIDGE

69

Whistler Mountain

Peak Chair - Glacier Bowl

The business! Arguably the best lift on the continent for spinning laps on steep alpine terrain. This is the principal lift for accessing Glacier Bowl, Whistler Bowl, West Bowl, and Bagel Bowl.

Glacier Bowl

An awesome wind-protected bowl with several entry options. To access Glacier Bowl, head left off the top of the chair and glide along Matthew's Traverse (Green) until you see a sign directing you (skier's left) to the run of your choice. All lines can be ridden back to the bottom of the Peak Chair!

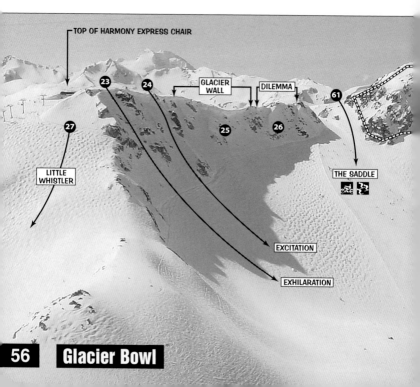

TOP OF HARMONY EXPRESS CHAIR

GLACIER WALL

DILEMMA

LITTLE WHISTLER

THE SADDLE

EXCITATION

EXHILARATION

Peak Chair - Glacier Bowl

59. The Cirque ....

Sideslip your way down an ugly, rocky ramp to what is often the most wind-protected section of Glacier Bowl. Additional photo on page 54.

60. The Couloir ....

Steep skiing into the heart of the bowl. Many people call The Couloir their favorite run on Whistler. Additional photo on page 54.

61. The Saddle ....

The ski area has gone to great lengths to open The Saddle up to the intermediate rider. Blasting at the ridge-top has created a more open entrance and allowed for regular grooming. Additional photos on pages 39 & 54.

TOP OF PEAK CHAIR

ENTRANCE HIDDEN BY ROCKS

Permanently Closed Area

THE CIRQUE

THE COULOIR

Peak Chair - Whistler Bowl

Classic, wide-open alpine terrain. All three entrances to Whistler Bowl are adjacent to the top of the Peak Chair.

62. Whistler Cornice. . . . .

As you approach the top of the chair, look to your left. You will see a cellular tower on top of a mound. On the other side of the mound (from the chair) is the entrance to Whistler Cornice.

63. Liftie's Leap. . . . .

A steep little roll behind the top lift shack.

64. Whistler Roll. . . . .

The widest-open access to the bowl. This entrance will set you up best for a descent down the heart of the bowl.

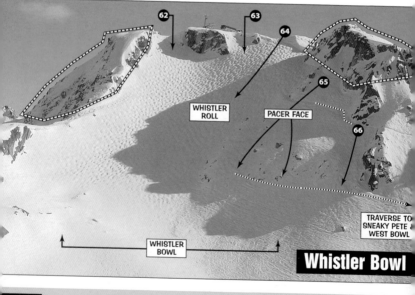

Whistler Bowl

TOP OF PEAK CHAIR

62

63

64

WHISTLER BOWL

65

66

67

Permanently Closed Area

PACER FACE

72

SNEAKY PETE

81

WEST CIRQUE

SUNRISE

68

68

UPPER V.D. CHUTES

77

GLOOM

DOOM

Peak Chair - Whistler Bowl

65. Pacer Face.
A steep, convex face. Traverse in from Whistler Roll Entrance.

66. Pacer Chute.
A steep, fall-line shot!

67. West Cirque.
Mega-classic steep face. Access the line by following Frontier Pass to the Permanent Closure fence above West Bowl. A short hike up along the fence line, back toward Whistler Bowl. Trust us—it's worth it! Additional photo on page 70.

68. Doom and Gloom.
Awesome varied terrain. Often neglected for more prominent lines. Photos on pages 59, 60 & 66.

69. Grande Finale.
The name says it all. A classy finish to Whistler Bowl. Additional photo on page 67.

Grande Finale

GLACIER BOWL

WHISTLER BOWL

UPPER V.D. CHUTES

77

68 68

69

GRANDE FINALE

HIGHWAY 86

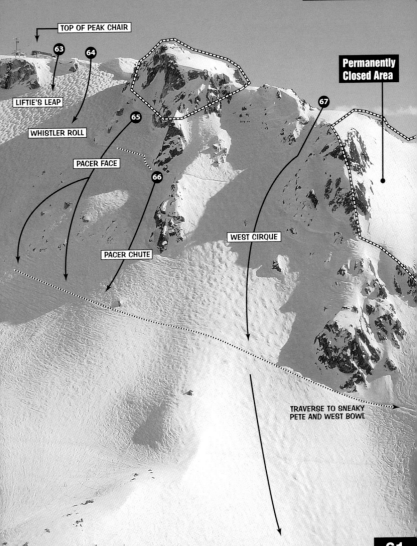

TOP OF PEAK CHAIR

63

64

Permanently
Closed Area

LIFTIE'S LEAP

65

67

WHISTLER ROLL

PACER FACE

66

WEST CIRQUE

PACER CHUTE

TRAVERSE TO SNEAKY
PETE AND WEST BOWL

WHISTLER BOWL

71

70

NORTH FACE LOW

SURPRISE

62

72

73

74

KEY WEST

SHALE CHUTE

SHALE SLOPE

PEAK CHAIR

Peak Chair - Lower Peak Chair Zone

The beauty of this zone is that all of the runs except Tigers Terrace and Upper V.D. Chutes will deposit you back at the base of the Peak Chair. The best access to this zone is via Whistler Bowl.

70. Surprise. . . . .
Awesome varied terrain. Bet you can't ride it the same way twice! To get to Surprise, stay skier's right in upper Whistler Bowl and look for signs directing you to pass under the Peak Chair lift line. Additional photo on page 54.

71. North Face Low. . . . .
A cool little drop under the Peak Chair lift line.

72. Shale Slope. . . . .
A true Whistler icon. After skiing the main slope of Whistler Bowl, head to the skier's right and look for signs directing you to Shale Slope. Use the Whistler Bowl overview photo as your guide. Additional photos on pages 54 and 59.

KEY WEST

SHALE CHUTE

SHALE SLOPE

LEFT HOOK

THE WATERFALL

73. Shale Chute . . . . ◆ ✦2 POW N ▢

Sometimes, due to the concavity of the terrain, the snow is a little more wind protected than it is on Shale Slope.

74. Key West . . . . ◆ ✦2 POW NE ▢

This line receives much less traffic than Shale Slope and, therefore, develops fewer moguls.

75. Left Hook . . . . ◆ ✦2 POW 🌲 N ▢

Gladed run beside Shale Slope. Sets you up for a launch off the Waterfall!

76. Tiger's Terrace . . . . ◆ ✦2 POW 🌲 NE ▢

Short but sweet tree lines. Often left alone by the hordes. After all, this is tiger country! Access this area by continuing along the ridge from the top of Shale Slope.

77. Upper V.D. Chutes . . . . ◆◆ ✦2 POW 🌲 NW ▢

Good glade skiing. Continue down the ridge above Tiger's Terrace and choose a line heading either down to Grand Finale or fall line to Highway 86 (Blue). Additional photos on pages 28, 59, 60 and 67.

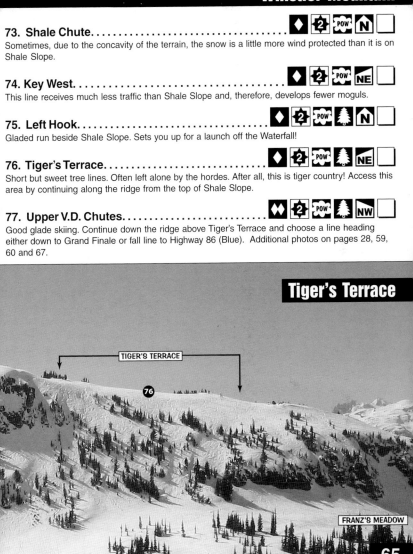

Tiger's Terrace

TIGER'S TERRACE

76

FRANZ'S MEADOW

BLACK TUSK

TRAVERSE TO
SNEAKY PETE

81

SUNRISE

82

ELEVATOR

83

ESCALATOR

68

DOOM & GLOOM

76

TIGER'S TERRACE

84

FROG HOLLOW

77

UPPER V.D. CHUTES

69

GRANDE
FINALE

Peak Chair - West Ridge

West Ridge is the ridge that divides Whistler Bowl and West Bowl. Access the ridge by taking Sneaky Pete's traverse from Whistler Bowl. The traverse will take you under Pacer Face and West Cirque to the top of West Ridge. See photo on page 61.

78. Sneaky Pete. . . . .
A popular entrance to West Bowl.

The following lines are accessed by riding along the top of West Ridge from the top of Sneaky Pete.

79. Everglades. . . . .
Some of the best tree skiing on either mountain. A great fall line through stunted trees.

WHISTLER BOWL

WEST BOWL

BAGEL BOWL

E

WEST RIDGE

W

78 FROG HOLLOW

80. Bonsai.

If Everglades is shredded, push your traverse over to Bonsai!

81. Sunrise.

A steep little chute. Not to be missed!

82. Elevator.

A very rocky line. It takes a lot of coverage before you can get any love in this elevator!

83. Escalator.

Going down!

84. Frog Hollow.

Good tree-skiing to Highway 86. Access by riding to the end of West Ridge from the top of Sneaky Pete.

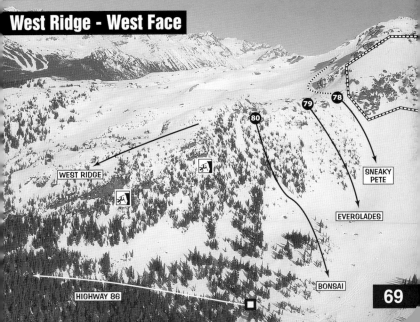

West Ridge - West Face

WEST RIDGE

SNEAKY PETE

EVERGLADES

BONSAI

HIGHWAY 86

69

WHISTLER BOWL

67

WEST CIRQUE

Permanently Closed Area

78

79

80

SNEAKY PETE

EVERGLADES

BONSAI

WEST RIDGE

84

FROG HOLLOW

70

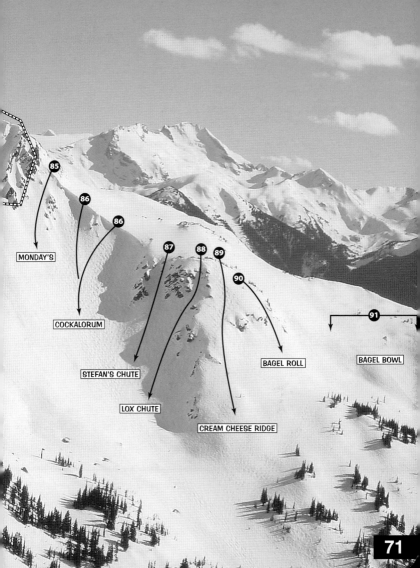

85

86

86

87

88

89

90

91

MONDAY'S

COCKALORUM

STEFAN'S CHUTE

LOX CHUTE

CREAM CHEESE RIDGE

BAGEL ROLL

BAGEL BOWL

Whistler Mountain

Peak Chair - West Bowl

An amazing expanse of alpine terrain. Access the bowl by taking Highway 86 (Blue) past its junction with Frontier Pass (Blue). After this point, on your right, will be a wind-scoured mass of crumbly rock. Slide over towards West Bowl around the downhill side of this rock.

85. Monday's.

The highest legal entrance into West Bowl.

86. Cockalorum.

This line often requires launching off a burly cornice.

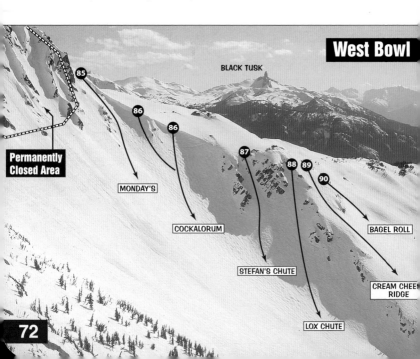

West Bowl

BLACK TUSK

Permanently Closed Area

MONDAY'S

COCKALORUM

STEFAN'S CHUTE

LOX CHUTE

BAGEL ROLL

CREAM CHEESE RIDGE

87. Stefan's Chute....................................
A classic, steep line that drops into the bowl.

88. Lox Chute..
Very similar to Stefan's.

89. Cream Cheese Ridge.............................
Often wind-affected.

90. Bagel Roll......................................
A steep convex roll on the end of the ridge between West Bowl and Bagel Bowl.

91. Bagel Bowl......................................
Good terrain, although it offers significantly less vertical for your effort.

92. Bernie's Bumps.................................
A few interesting rolls, but pretty lame terrain overall. Sorry, Bernie!

Bagel Bowl

NDAY'S

COCKALORUM

STEFAN'S CHUTE

LOX CHUTE

BAGEL ROLL

CREAM CHEESE RIDGE

BAGEL BOWL

BERNIE'S BUMPS

HIGHWAY 86

Peak Chair - Peak to Creek

An expansion in 2004 added 1,100 new acres of terrain on Whistler Mountain.

93. Peak to Creek. . . . .
Whistler Blackcomb threw a few million dollars into "summer grooming" some of the rough spots on this big new cruiser. The result is a 5020' descent that will see periodic grooming throughout the winter. I hope you've been using your Thighmaster!

94. Big Timber. . . . .
Much like Peak to Creek except it's been left with all the natural rolls, drops and ground cover. This is sure to keep the local skiers interested and coming back for more.

95. Dusty's Descent. . . . .
Another new option in the Creekside leading you right to the watering hole of the same name. If you have not done après at Dusty's, then you have not done après!

96. Home Run. . . . .
A shorter option that winds its way to the housing developments on the south side.

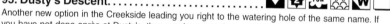
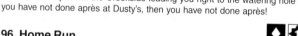

LOOKING DOWN LOWER PEAK TO CREEK FROM ABOVE HIGHWAY 86

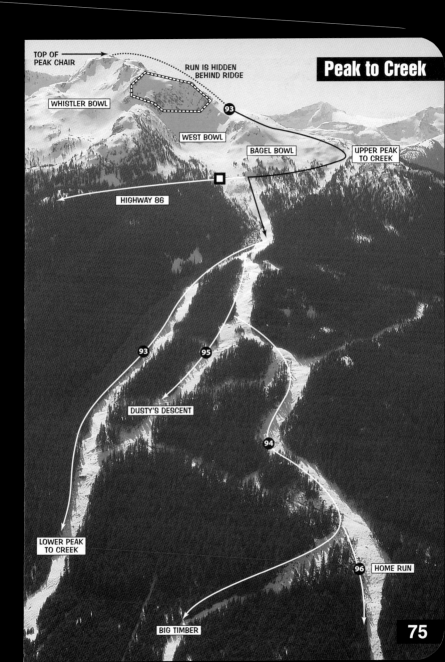

Zip from Whistler to Blackcomb at up to 80 km/hour

Three hour guided zipline eco-adventures include five ziplines, canopy bridges and a snowcat ride to Ziptrek's base on Blackcomb Mountain. Day and evening tours depart hourly from the Carleton Lodge across from the Village Gondolas. Open 365 days a year.

ZIPTREK & TREETREK
ECOTOURS
604.935.0001
Toll Free 1.866.935.0001
www.ziptrek.com

SnowCovers

www.snowcovers.com

BLACKCOMB
GLACIER

HORSTMAN
GLACIER

SECRET
BASIN

CRYSTAL RIDGE

FRAGGLE ROCK

JERSEY CREAM

BLACKCOMB GLACIER ROAD

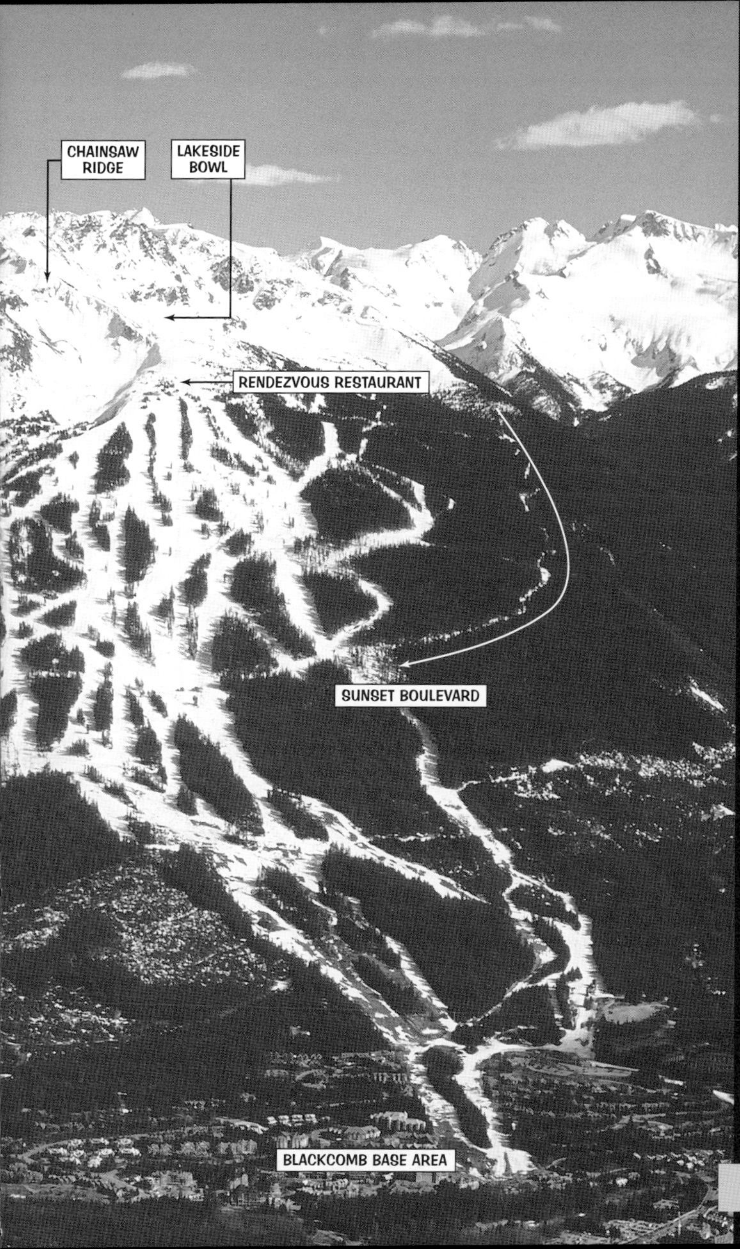

CHAINSAW RIDGE

LAKESIDE BOWL

RENDEZVOUS RESTAURANT

SUNSET BOULEVARD

BLACKCOMB BASE AREA

BLACKCOMB

Blackcomb - Vertical Chart

	Village	Daylodge	Base 2	Excelerator	Wizard Top
Village	0	n/a	279'	1493'	1882'
Daylodge	n/a	0	246'	1460'	1849'
Base 2	279'	246'	0	1214'	1603'
Excelerator	1493'	1460'	1214'	0	389'
Wizard Top	1882'	1849'	1603'	389'	0
Rendezvous	3888'	3855'	3669'	2395'	2066'
Glacier Creek	2855'	2822'	2576'	1362'	1000'
Crystal Hut	3839'	3806'	3560'	2346'	1957'
Horstman Hut	5280'	5247'	5001'	3787'	3398'
Blowhole	5253'	5220'	4974'	3760'	3371'
Spanky's	4691'	4658'	4412'	3198'	2809'

Rendezvous	Glacier Creek	Crystal Hut	Horstman Hut	Blowhole	Spanky's
3888'	2855'	3839'	5280'	5253'	4691'
3855'	2822'	3806'	5247'	5220'	4658'
3669'	2576'	3560'	5001'	4974'	4412'
2395'	1362'	2346'	3787'	3760'	3198'
2066'	1000'	1957'	3398'	3371'	2809'
0	1033'	n/a	1392'	n/a	n/a
1033'	0	984'	2425'	2398'	1836'
n/a	984'	0	1441'	1414'	852'
1392'	2425'	1441'	0	n/a	589'
n/a	2398'	1414'	n/a	0	562'
n/a	1836'	852'	589'	562'	0

Blackcomb images clockwise from far left: shredding the steeps, Teetering Rock, skier and rider hiking for the goods and snow rime on Horstman Hut.

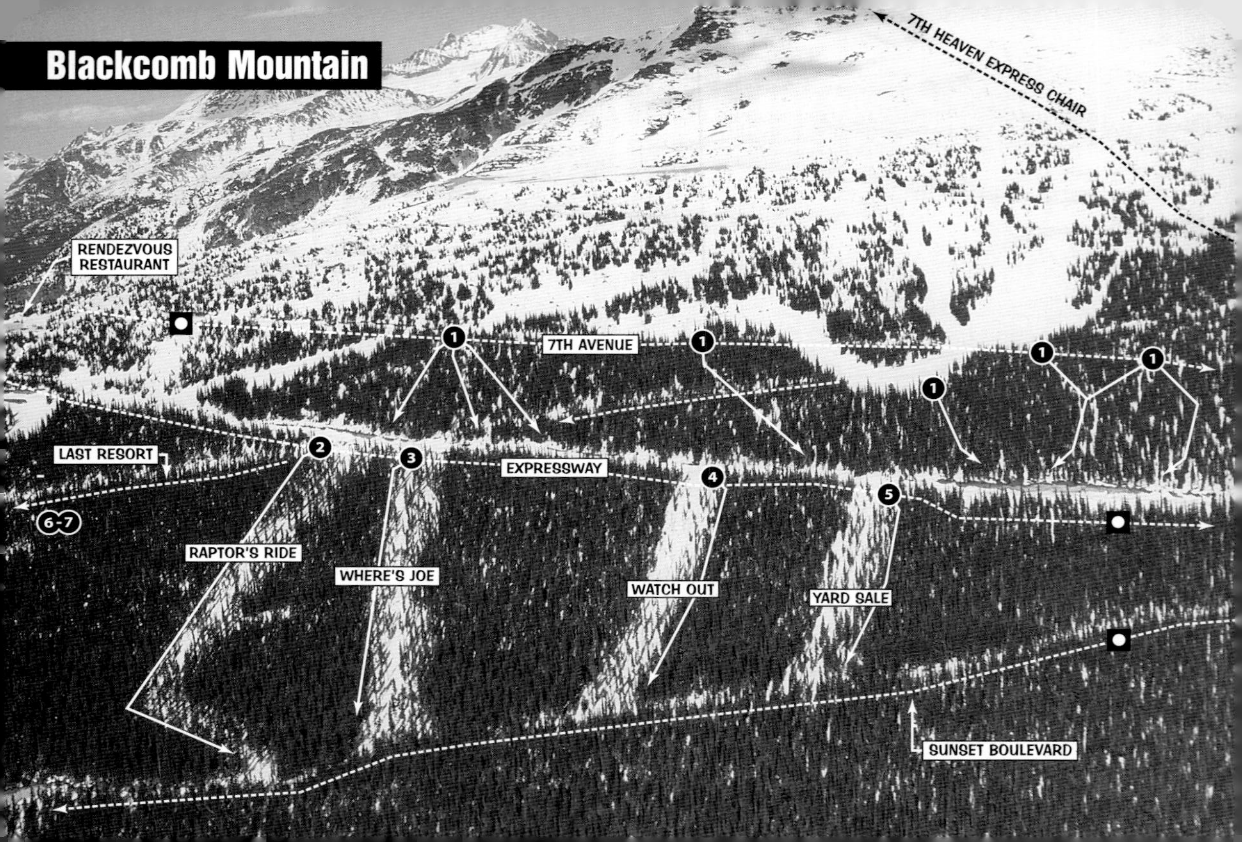
Blackcomb Mountain
7TH HEAVEN EXPRESS CHAIR
RENDEZVOUS RESTAURANT
7TH AVENUE
1
2
3
4
5
LAST RESORT
EXPRESSWAY
6-7
RAPTOR'S RIDE
WHERE'S JOE
WATCH OUT
YARD SALE
SUNSET BOULEVARD

Solar Coaster Express Chair - Sub-Alpine Terrain

Even in the most heinous storms, when the high alpine remains closed, there is lots of terrain on Blackcomb that beats sitting at home with your PlayStation 2. Check these out:

1. Lines off 7ᵗʰ Avenue ..... ◆ ■ 2 POW ♠ SW □

There are some short, steep lines that drop off 7ᵗʰ Avenue through tight trees to Express Way below.

2. Raptor's Ride ..... ◆ ■ 1 POW ♠ SW □

These are the gladed runs off Expressway. These four runs are very similar in nature but can provide several runs worth of entertainment.

3. Where's Joe ..... ◆ ■ 1 POW ♠ SW □

4. Watch Out ..... ◆ ■ 1 POW ♠ SW □

5. Yard Sale ..... ◆ ■ 1 POW ♠ SW □

6. Renegade Glade ..... ◆ ■ 2 POW ♠ W □

Renegade Glade and Little Cub are two often neglected glade runs found off Last Resort. The Patrol loves these runs because they sometimes have untouched powder left at the end of the day for sweep!

7. Little Cub ..... ◆ ■ 2 POW ♠ W □

Renegade Glade

Jersey Cream Express Chair - Sub-Alpine Terrain

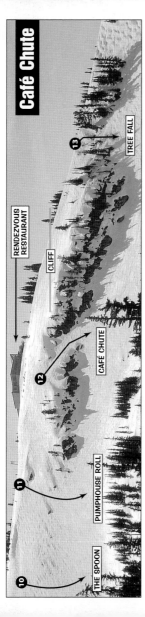

This sub-alpine area is usually one of the first zones to get avalanche clearance. It can be opened even if there is active avalanche control being conducted on the alpine slopes above. The area offers some short but fun chutes, small drops, and a traverse out to some good glades and steeps.

8. Hot Tub . . . .
Short little convex slope off the top of Jersey Cream Express Chair. Named after the round hot-tub-looking water tower.

9. Jersey Cream Wall . . . .
The headwall pitch below the top three towers of the Jersey Cream Express Chair. Watch for the rocks!

Café Chute

10. The Spoon . . . .
A small scooped bowl on the left side of the Jersey Cream Wall.

11. Pumphouse Roll . . . .
Headwall roll above the snowmaking house. Watch those rocks!

12. Café Chute . . . .
Fun little diagonal chute directly below the restaurant. Some drop the lower cliff on deep days; make sure you stick the landing, because everyone on the chair *is* watching!

13. Tree Fall . . . .
Final short chute on the "Café Wall", 200 meters skier's left of Café Chute, squeezed between the cliff and the tree-island.

HEAVENLY BASIN

34

35

HAOLE
ROCK

DAKINE

BAGGERS

16

19

STAIRCASE

GLACIER
DRIVE

THE BITE

JERSEY CREAM EXPRESS CHAIR

GLACIER EXPRESS CHAIR

Jersey Cream Overview

32

COUGAR CHUTES

HIGH TRAVERSE

15

14

COYOTE ROAD

CAFÉ CLIFFS

18

17

JERSEY CREAM RUN

BLOWDOWN

Blackcomb Mountain

 Jersey Cream Express - Sub-Alpine Terrain

The next four lines are found off the Coyote Road. Coyote Road is the name of an old road that traverses from Jersey Cream Run to Glacier Drive. Originally put in for the construction of the Glacier Express Chair, it is groomed periodically and provides a gliding traverse to several good steep boulder strewn runs. Ski off the top of the Jersey Cream Chair on Jersey Cream Run's right side. Enter the gate at the bottom of the Cougar fence and traverse to the right until you hit the Coyote Road below.

14. Bagger 1 . . . .

The short boulder-filled area just above the road is known as the Baggers and has a few sweet lines.

28

30

TEETERING

PAKALOLO

GLACIER EXPRESS CHAIR

HAOLE ROCK

15. Bagger 2 . . . . ◆ 2 POW N 𝍏

16. Bagger 3 . . . . ◆ 2 POW N 𝍏

17. Blowdown . . . . ◆ 1 🕸 N

Steep bowl below Coyote Road consisting of two rocky knolls with a variety of fun chutes. This terrain is used as the qualifying grounds for the Big Mountain Experience and the World Extreme Championships.

18. Staircase . . . . ◆ 1 🕸 N

19. The Bite . . . . ◆ 1 🕸 N

Baggers / Café Chute

RENDEZVOUS RESTAURANT

CAFÉ CLIFFS

14
15
16

THE BAGGERS

Victoria Jealouse big wave surfing Whistler style. Photo: Bryn Hughes

Chris Eby chases his shadow in Whistler's Sunbowl. Photo: Damian Cromwell

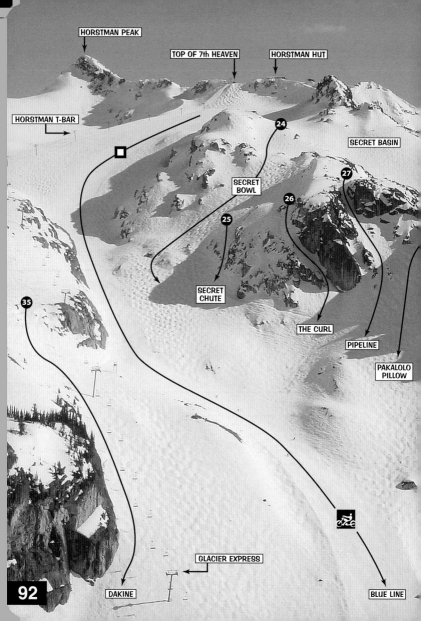

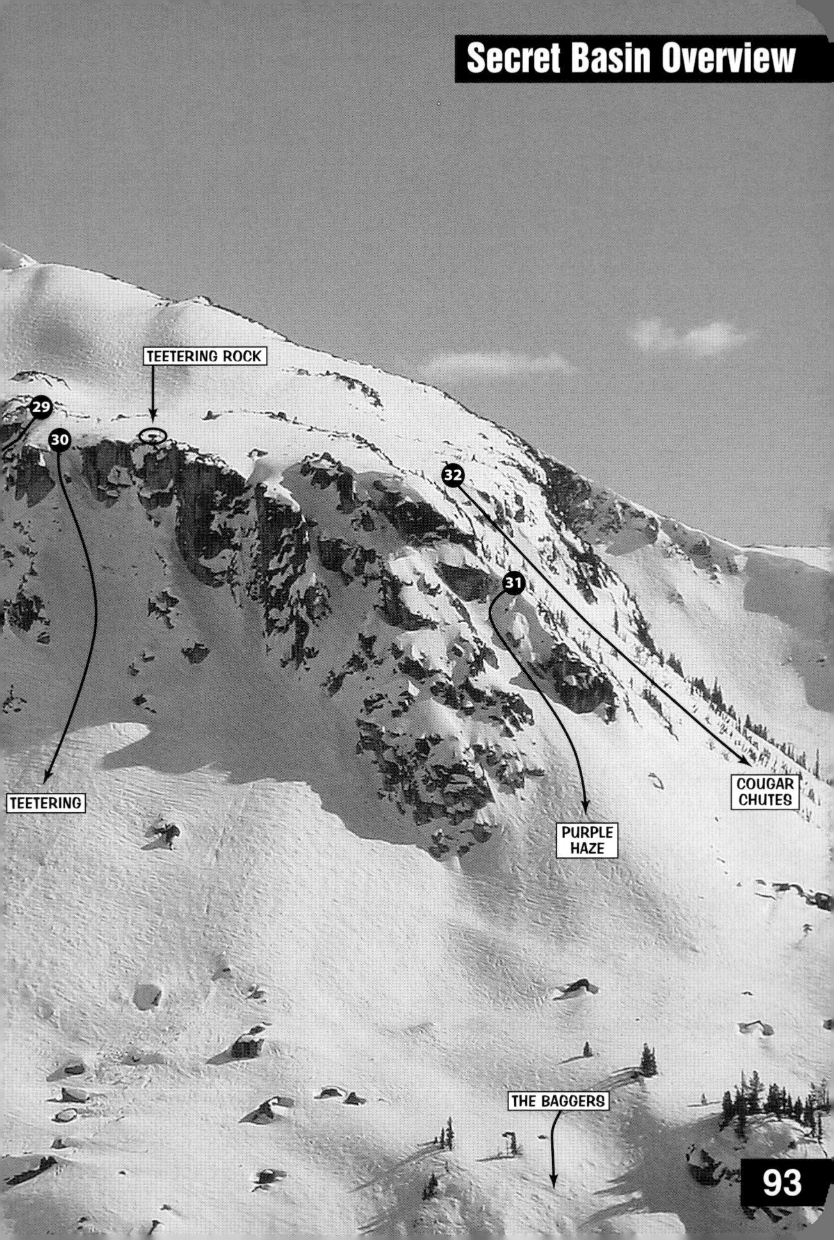

TEETERING ROCK

29

30

32

31

TEETERING

PURPLE HAZE

COUGAR CHUTES

THE BAGGERS

Glacier Express Chair - Secret Basin

The Swiss Cheese area is the craggy terrain to the skier's right of Secret Bowl. This complex little area can offer great skiing, once you are familiar with it. Access is via traverse from the top of Glacier Express into the Secret Basin.

20. Clean Out . . . .
Pick your way through the granite to the top of the Swiss massive. Follow the blunt ridge until it is possible to slide into the flat slope. Funnel into Secret Bowl.

21. My Line . . . .
My Line works its way through the rocks on the left side of Swiss Cheese, eventually merging with Secret Basin. Start high or via Clean Out.

22. Circle Chute . . . .
Work your way skier's right, through the labyrinth, and hop down a few short cliffs to gain Circle Chute.

Swiss Cheese

HORSTMAN HUT

SWISS CHEESE

MY LINE

CLEAN OUT

SECRET BOWL

BLUE LINE

CIRCLE CHUTE

23. Swiss Cheese . . . .

The run Swiss Cheese is a big piece of terrain with short little pitches of riding through cliffs. The best way to find a good line is to scope the terrain from the Glacier Express chair before exploring. Additional photo on page 117.

24. Secret Bowl . . . .

From Secret Basin, follow the natural line into the saddle between Swiss Cheese and Secret Basin.

25. Secret Chute . . . .

Ski the left side of Secret Bowl and watch for the chute that develops in the lower third of the bowl.

26. The Curl . . . .

Known to some as Lone Pine, for the one little tree that grows at the bottom.

27. Pipeline . . . .

Access via Pakalolo and traverse right as high as you can. Several variations are possible.

SECRET BASIN

Pakalolo

TEETERING ROCK

PAKALOLO

PIPELINE

THE CURL

TEETERING

Glacier Express Chair - Secret Basin

28. Pakalolo . . . .

Traverse to Secret Basin, but stay left of the bowl and look for the obvious entrance into this classic couloir. Additional photo on page 88.

29. Pakalolo Pillow . . . .

The burlier entrance into the couloir. Stay even farther left and work your way around the rocks to gain access to the edge of the drop in.

30. Teetering . . . .

Named after the Coyote rock, perched on the edge of the cliff 30 meters left, Teetering is the STEEP entrance into this chute. Access depends on snow coverage! Additional photo page 88.

Pakalolo

THE CURL

PIPELINE

TEETERING

Glacier Express Chair - Secret Basin

These steep chutes, visible from the top third of the Jersey Cream chair, are accessed via the Secret Basin and a continuous traverse left, past the sign line.

31. Purple Haze . . . .

Enter the top of the Cougar Chute Right and traverse right, on the flat bench with the two small islands of trees. Creep to the edge below the cornice and scope it out! Don't miss your first turn, because you might not get a second one!

32. Cougar Chutes. . . . .

Several lines are possible through the chutes and boulders. Watch for the "pungy trees"! Additional photos on pages 87 & 106.

Cougar Chutes

31
32
32

PURPLE HAZE

COUGAR CHUTES

Blackcomb Mountain

CHIMNEY BOOT-PACK TO GREY ZONE

GLACIER EXPRESS CHAIR

33

35

HEAVENLY BASIN

DAKINE

34

HAOLE ROCK

DON'T STOP

36

SMOKED SALMON

37

SALMON BELLY

38

OVERBITE

39

Glacier Express Chair - Crystal Traverse

From the top of Glacier Express, the Crystal Traverse (a.k.a. the Blue Road) offers the easiest way back to Crystal Hut. Off this road, there are several noteworthy descents.

33. Heavenly Basin.......... ◆ 🔲2️⃣ ❄ W

Find it just off the Crystal Road, past the hairpin turn. Large variation in aspect ensures quality snow.

34. Haole Rock.............. ◆ 🔲1️⃣ POW W

Skier's left in Heavenly Basin. The big rock outcrop is Haole Rock. This line is funky terrain between the thin trees and the rock. Additional photo on page 86.

35. Dakine.......... ◆ 🔲2️⃣ N ⬝⬝⬝

This refers to the line skier's left of the huge Haole rock, under the chair. Additional photos on pages 86 and 92.

36. Don't Stop........... ◆ 🔲3️⃣ POW W

Past Heavenly Basin, there are three great lines off the Crystal Road, before you reach the Crystal Hut restaurant. First comes Don't Stop, the killer S-shaped chute through the trees.

37. Smoked Salmon........ ◆ 🔲3️⃣ POW W

The second chute through the trees and the most sustained of the three.

38. Salmon Belly......... ◆ 🔲2️⃣ POW W

The third route, closest to the Hot Rocks cliff face, the Belly widens out below the cliff and has room for more fresh lines.

39. Overbite.............. ◆ 🔲1️⃣ W ⬝⬝⬝

This cut run is chronically rocky and is best avoided unless it is a 30-centimeter-plus day!

40. Davies Dervish........ ⬝⬝⬝ ◆ 🔲2️⃣

This mogul horror show is the site of all the World Cup mogul events. Call your physiotherapist for an appointment before you drop in! Still interested? Access is off Blueline.

Permanently Closed Area

OPAL BOWL

46

ROMPER ROOM

45

RIDGE RUNNER

CBC

CHIMNEY
BOOTPACK

41

THE GREY ZONE

42

43

44

CRYSTAL HUT & TOP
OF CRYSTAL CHAIR

MOLLY'S
REACH

DANGER
BAY

FRONT PAGE
CHALLENGE

FRAGGLE
ROCK

47

TO ARTHUR'S CHOICE, LOG
JAM & OUTER LIMITS

Blackcomb Mountain

This high-alpine ridge and bowl sit above the Crystal Chair. Access to these slopes is best made via "The Chimney", a bootpack above the Crystal Traverse. To find it, follow the Crystal Traverse from the top of Glacier Express for 1,200 meters, until the sharp left corner. Leave the road and traverse the boulder-strewn upper Heavenly Basin to the short hike below the cliffs at the first tree island (see page 98).

41. The Grey Zone . . . .
From the top of The Chimney bootpack, descend this wide ridge to the Crystal Hut. Great lower-angle powder skiing. Watch for boulders!

42. Molly's Reach . . . .
Cross the Grey Zone to the fence on skier's right. Follow the fence to the end and approach the edge carefully to find a way in.

43. Danger Bay . . . .
Same as Molly's, only traverse the ridge farther and find your way into the chute from right to left.

44. Front Page Challenge . . . .
The lowest and easiest way into the Opal Bowl before you reach the traverse in from Crystal Chair. Take this line first and scope out the others.

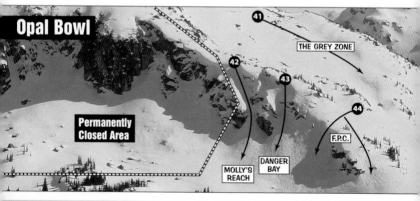

Opal Bowl

THE GREY ZONE

Permanently Closed Area

F.P.C.

MOLLY'S REACH

DANGER BAY

Rider: Victoria Jealouse   Photo: Bryn Hughes

Crystal Chair - Fraggle Rock

This old lift runs slow and preserves powder. It also offers great cruising and tree skiing. In big storms, it is often the highest lift open. Don't miss the waffles served in the restaurant at the top!

45. CBC
Traverse across Opal Bowl to the tree line. This area is a very complex maze of cliffs, frozen waterfalls, and chutes. Don't go in there without an experienced guide!

46. Romper Room
Traverse across Opal Bowl toward the trees. When you hit the boundary disks, turn downhill and shred the fun rolling terrain. Traverse left after 200 meters, to get back to Ridge Runner.

47. Fraggle Rock
Follow the Crystal Road below Crystal Hut. At the right turn where the road veers away from Rock 'n' Roll to Ridge Runner, you can access the bootpack up to Fraggle Rock. This rocky varied terrain is like a natural terrain park. There are three lines—left, center and right—all of which are worth a look.

48. Outer Limits (no photo)
The only Double-Black-Diamond gladed run on either mountain. It can be heaven or hell, depending on the snow. Access is through the big wooden gate on the skier's right of Ridge Runner.

49. Arthur's Choice / Log Jam / Rider's Revenge
These glades are the same as Outer Limits, but less steep. Definitely worth a look when the snow is good. Log Jam and Rider's Revenge are not visible in any of the photos.

HORSTMAN PEAK

Fraggle Rock

TOP OF CHIMNEY BOOTPACK

SECRET BASIN

1

THE GREY ZONE

CRYSTAL HUT & TOP
OF CRYSTAL CHAIR

BOOT-
PACK

47 FRAGGLE
ROCK

RIDGE
RUNNER

49

ARTHUR'S CHOICE

BACKSTAGE
PASS

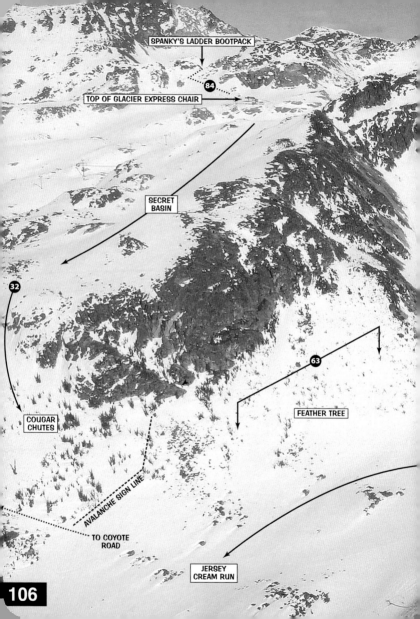

SPANKY'S LADDER BOOTPACK

84

TOP OF GLACIER EXPRESS CHAIR

SECRET BASIN

32

63

COUGAR CHUTES

FEATHER TREE

AVALANCHE SIGN LINE

TO COYOTE ROAD

JERSEY CREAM RUN

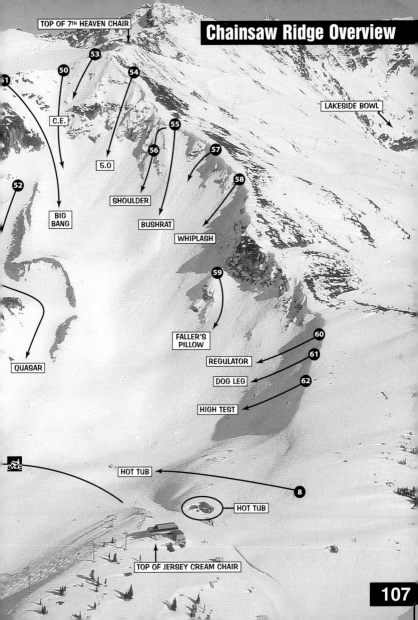

TOP OF 7TH HEAVEN CHAIR

53

50

54

LAKESIDE BOWL

1

C.E.

55

56

57

5.0

52

58

SHOULDER

BIG
BANG

BUSHRAT

WHIPLASH

59

QUASAR

FALLER'S
PILLOW

60

REGULATOR

61

DOG LEG

62

HIGH TEST

HOT TUB

8

HOT TUB

TOP OF JERSEY CREAM CHAIR

Blackcomb Mountain

HAWAII 5.0

EXPOSED TRAVERSES

COULOUR EXTREME

QUASAR

FALSE FACE

BIG BANG

7th Heaven Express Chair - Chainsaw Ridge

The gateway to Blackcomb's high alpine. The 7th Heaven chair accesses the ridge that divides the Horstman Glacier to the north and Lakeside and Jersey Cream Bowl to the south. With amazing terrain in every direction, 7th Heaven allows you to access whatever you are looking for.

Chainsaw Ridge

The showpiece steeps visible from the Rendezvous restaurant. Home of the famous Couloir Extreme. Access via the lookout north of the Horstman Hut restaurant.

50. Couloir Extreme

An ultra-popular mega-couloir. The line is right down the center of the bowl. Formerly known as the Saudan Couloir, this has been the staging place for the thigh-burning horror show known as the Couloir Extreme race. Don't forget to buy the T-shirt.

51. Big Bang

Think of it as the Couloir's little brother. Ski in 50 feet right of the entrance to the Couloir Extreme main chute. Work the terrain left of the rocky moraine in the bowl. Also known as "Sylvain".

52. Quasar

The easiest line in the zone. Sneak into the bowl at the farthest-right gate and work the slope on the skier's right of the lateral moraine.

53. False Face

Serious mountain terrain that's not for the faint of heart, this line could be one of the steepest skiable faces at any ski area in North America.

54. Hawaii 5-0

Skiing for the ultra-hardcore. Don't fall!

7th Heaven Express Chair - Chainsaw Ridge 109

7th Heaven Express Chair - Chainsaw Ridge

55. Bushrat . . . .

Ski down the ridge about halfway, to the obvious notch entrance in the cornice. Then, drop in and ski the diagonal chute or shoulder.

56. Bushrat Shoulder . . . .

Bushrat Shoulder shares the same entrance as Bushrat proper. Once you are in the bowl, ride the shoulder fall line below and skier's right of the main chute.

57. Bushwhip . . . .

Sandwiched between Bushrat and Whiplash lies Bushwhip. The entrance can be tricky and very dangerous depending on how the cornice forms. Scope it from below first!

58. Whiplash . . . .

Sometimes this line goes and sometimes it doesn't, depending on the cornice. Scope it out from below, before you try to find a way in!

59. Fallers Pillow . . . .

This slope is on the skier's left of the cliffs, in the middle of the bowl. Often the deepest snow in the bowl. Bring your snorkel!

Bushrat

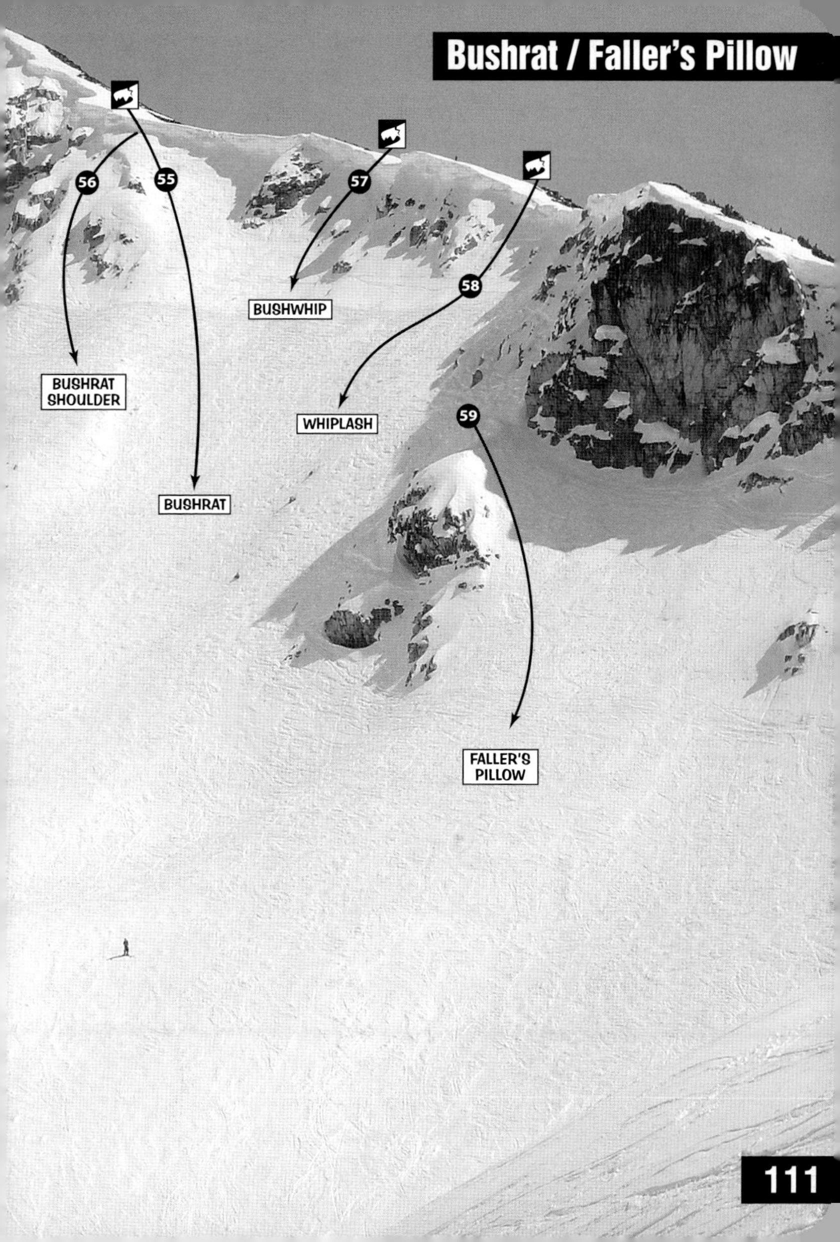

56

55

57

58

59

BUSHWHIP

BUSHRAT
SHOULDER

WHIPLASH

BUSHRAT

FALLER'S
PILLOW

7th Heaven Express Chair - Chainsaw Ridge

60. Regulator . . . .

The lower third of the ridge starts with this open line. Would-be Whistler Extreme-O's should consider this their first cornice drop and right of passage.

60

60

61

REGULATOR

DOG LEG

61. Dog Leg ....

The crooked line down hill from the Regulator cornice.

62. High Test / Low Test ....

Two convex rolls at the bottom of the ridge.

63. Feather Tree ....

Feather Tree is the name given to the slope below the cliffs between Cougar Chutes and Quasar. Access can be gained via traverse in from either side. See photo on page 106.

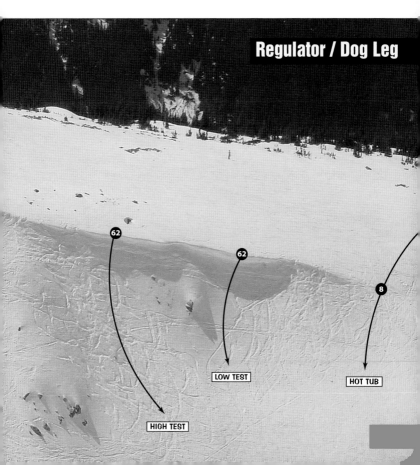

Regulator / Dog Leg

62
62
8
LOW TEST
HOT TUB
HIGH TEST

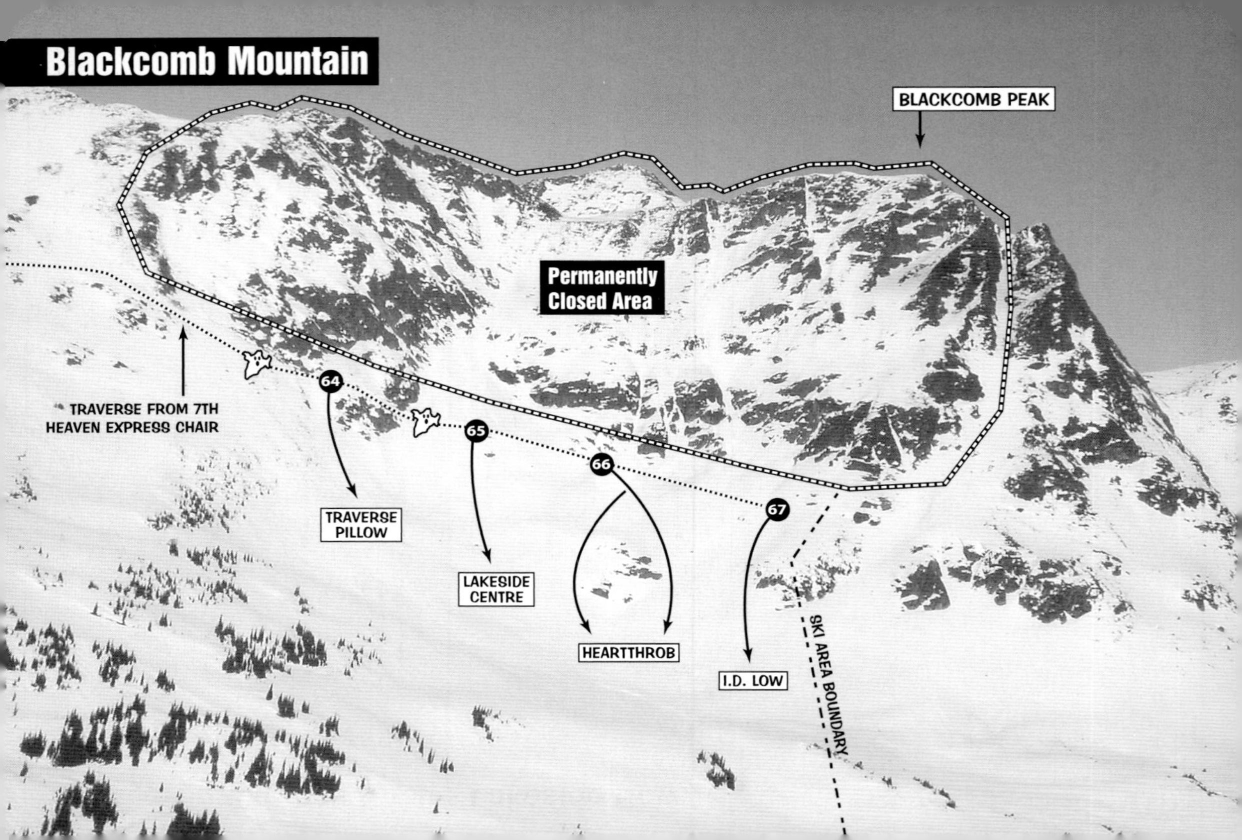

Blackcomb Mountain

BLACKCOMB PEAK

SKI AREA BOUNDARY

67 I.D. LOW

66 HEARTTHROB

Permanently Closed Area

65 LAKESIDE CENTRE

TRAVERSE PILLOW

64

TRAVERSE FROM 7TH HEAVEN EXPRESS CHAIR

7th Heaven Express Chair - Lakeside Bowl

This is the massive bowl visible as you ride up the 7th Heaven Chair. Get off at the top and head right along the Green Line to the first corner. Continue traversing to the fence line and enter a gate to Lakeside Bowl. The traverse is Triple-Black-Diamond and can be more hazardous than any of the actual skiing!

64. Traverse Pillow

Once you enter through the gate and take the high traverse toward the bowl, you reach a point where you can sidestep up under a ski-patrol bomb tram. This slope is the Pillow, and when skied from below the cliffs, it makes for quick access to good powder.

65. Lakeside Center

Traverse to the center of the massive bowl and rip it up! Don't even think of hiking above the traverse, because it is a Permanent Closure and you will lose your pass!

66. Heartthrob

The small rock outcrop mid-bowl is known as Heartthrob. Ski across the top and shred the left or right side.

67. I.D. Low

Continue the rising traverse across the bowl, stepping up over a lateral cornice. Ski back in and air if you dare! Great powder lies below the fan.

Joe Lammers makes his own waterfall on Blackcomb's Ladies First. Photo: Damian Cromwell

TOP OF SHOWCASE T-BAR

BLACKCOMB GLACIER

Permanently Closed Area

84

SPANKY'S LADDER

TOP OF GLACIER EXPRESS CHAIR

116

Horstman Glacier Overview

HORSTMAN PEAK

STUPIDS

TOP OF HORSTMAN T-BAR

TOP OF 7TH HEAVEN EXPRESS

HORSTMAN HUT

HORSTMAN GLACIER

BLUE LINE

23

SWISS CHEESE

7th Heaven Express Chair - Horstman Peak

The ridge rising above the 7th Heaven Chair reaches Horstman peak above the Blowhole and Blackcomb Glacier. The lower-angled south side is visible as you ride up the 7th Heaven Chair, and the steeper skiable terrain on the north side is described below. Access is gained by walking behind the top tower of the Horstman T-bar to gain the bootpack onto the ridge. Ski lines are described as you meet them.

68. Jump For Joy ....
The first skiable face that you get to on the ridge. Short and steep. If *you* feel sketchy, just think about the guy who successfully rode his mountain bike down this for a Warren Miller movie!

69. Prime Rib ....
The steep convex slope gained by hiking up from the first corner of the Blue road. Some simply ride in off the corner of the road, but for full value, hike to the ridge. FYI: This point is where the top of the original 7th Heaven T-bar had it's unload!

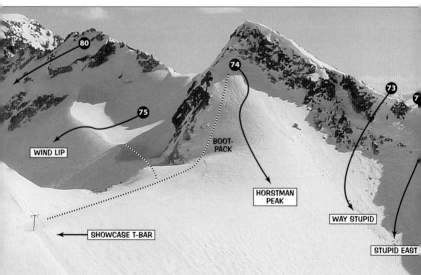

70. Pearly Gates . . . .

The first line off the upper half of the ridge. To see in, you have to walk uphill a ways. Entrance varies, depending on the size of the cornice.

71. Stupid West . . . .

Off-angle line that picks its way through the rocks. Only fills in when there is lots of snow.

72. Stupid East . . . .

The best on the ridge. Gives you a nice line into the bowl. The way in under the cornice is usually from right to left. This steep headwall finishes with a nice wide fan at the bottom.

73. Way Stupid . . . .

This chute is only skiable in the fattest conditions. The problem is that when conditions are fat, so is the cornice! Most people traverse in from Stupid East.

74. Horstman Peak . . . .

This slope is the big powder fan that builds up under the north face of the Peak. Access is gained by riding the Showcase T-bar, traversing over and bootpacking up the fan.

Horstman Peak

STUPID WEST

PEARLY GATES

PRIME RIB

JUMP FOR JOY

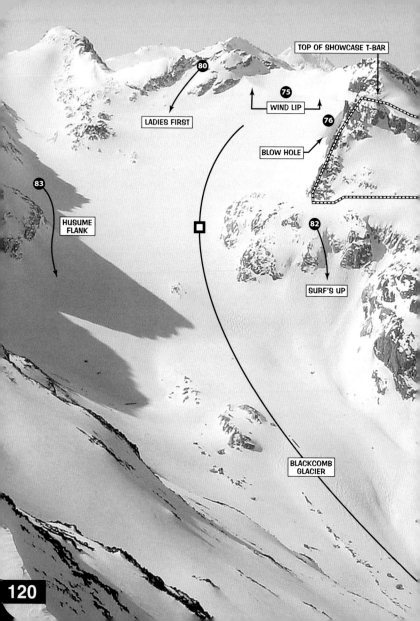

TOP OF SHOWCASE T-BAR

80

75

WIND LIP

76

LADIES FIRST

BLOW HOLE

83

HUSUME FLANK

82

SURF'S UP

BLACKCOMB GLACIER

HORSTMAN GLACIER

Permanently Closed Area

TOP OF SPANKY'S LADDER BOOTPACK

GARNET BOWL

SAPPHIRE BOWL

DIAMOND BOWL

HUSUME
FLANK

BLACKCOMB
GLACIER

TOP OF SHOWCASE T-BAR &
BLACKCOMB GLACIER ENTRANCE

SAPPHIRE
BOWL

DIAMOND
BOWL

RUBY
BOWL

OPAL
BOWL

**Permanently
Closed Area**

SKI OUT

123

Blackcomb Mountain

 Showcase T-Bar - Blackcomb Glacier

The highest lift on the mountain, Showcase T-Bar accesses the Blackcomb Glacier and the world-famous Wind Lip. In major storms, this lift will stay closed in order to keep people out of the massive terrain behind the ridge, which often experiences avalanches up to Class 4 in size!

75. The Wind Lip . . . .
The Wind Lip is a giant snow moat created by the force of the wind that comes over the ridge. This, combined with the steep slope below, makes it the best natural booter in the world! Made famous in countless ski and snowboard movies, this is a must-do for any would-be huckster. Additional photo on page 118.

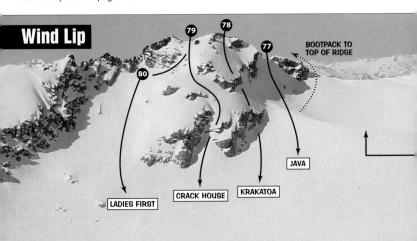

Wind Lip

BOOTPACK TO
TOP OF RIDGE

JAVA

LADIES FIRST

CRACK HOUSE

KRAKATOA

TO HUSUME FLANK

76. The Blowhole ....

Get off the Showcase T-Bar and traverse to the right for 50 meters, to a place where you can bootpack up to the Blackcomb Glacier gate. Once through the gate this huge feature is on your left. To capture the glory, have your photographer shoot from the ridge behind the wooden sign or from the bottom, looking up.

77. Java ....

Hike along the Wind Lip and climb to the ridge. Traverse around the rocks and up to a chute. Ski back into the glacier watching carefully for crevasses!

78. Krakatoa ....

Access as above. Hike around the back of the rock ridge to the top. Serious cornice hazard! This run involves drops over two rock bands that can be 6 feet or 36 feet depending on snow cover!

79. Crack House ....

Hike to the top as for Ladies First. Negotiate around the upper cliff to the chute with mandatory air!

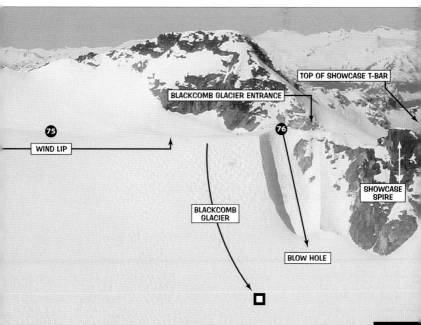

Showcase T-Bar - Blackcomb Glacier

80. Ladies First . . . .
Continue along the rock ridge - past the notch, over the top, and in near the Permanent Closure fence that is placed here for keeping skiers out of Upper Lakeside Bowl. Sometimes, you have to carry your boards down and right, over some rocks. Additional photo on page 118.

81. Winky Pop . . . .
Traverse left through the labyrinth of rocks, on the wide bench below the Blowhole.

82. Surf's Up . . . .
Access is the same as for Winky Pop, only sidestep up a further 10 to 15 meters to gain the chute at the top of Surf's Up.

83. Husume Flank . . . .
Great link up from Ladies First. Traverse to the right side of Blackcomb Glacier. The Flank line runs down the fan below all the cliffs. Additional photo on page 120.

Husume

SKI AREA BOUNDARY

83

HUSUME FLANK

BLACKCOMB GLACIER

ENTRANCE TO BLACKCOMB GLACIER

TOP OF SHOWCASE T-BAR

Surf's Up

76

BLOW HOLE

Permanently
Closed Area

TO SAPPHIRE BOWL

81   82

SURF'S UP

WINKY POP

BLACKCOMB GLACIER

ENTRANCE TO BLACKCOMB GLACIER

TOP OF SHOWCASE T-BAR

BLOW HOLE

HORSTMAN GLACIER

76

Permanently Closed Area

TOP OF SPANKY'S LADDER BOOTPACK

82

85

86

GARNET BOWL

SURF'S UP

SAPPHIRE BOWL

90

DIAMOND BOWL

SAPPHIRE CHUTES

9

BLACKCOMB GLACIER

Gemstone Bowls Overview

WHISTLER MOUNTAIN

98

SPANKY'S SHOULDER

Permanently Closed Area

RUBY BOWL

MID-BOWL ROLL

Blackcomb Mountain

The Glacier Express Chair takes you from the "Jersey Cream Flats" (outside of the Glacier Creek mega-restaurant) up to the bottom of the Horstman Glacier and the two T-bars. It is also the gateway to Spanky's Ladder bootpack and the Gemstone Bowls of Garnet, Ruby, Diamond, and Sapphire. In some storms, this is the highest lift open on the mountain, and Spanky's Ladder may remain closed. If this is the case, there is still plenty of high-alpine terrain in the Cougar and Secret areas.

84. Spanky's Ladder . . . .

No easy way out from here! Spanky's Ladder is the 15 meter bootpack that you must hike to access the ridge between Crystal Traverse and the Blackcomb Glacier valley. Get off Glacier Express and turn left, traverse below the ridge for 400 meters to the bottom of a steep snow slope. From here, hike up and through the gate. Additional photos on pages 106 and 116.

85. Garnet Bowl . . . .

Garnet is the upper basin that funnels you into Sapphire, Diamond, and Ruby Bowls. From the gate at the top of Spanky's Ladder, a traverse to the right leads to Sapphire Bowl, to the left leads to Ruby, and if you go straight, you end up in Diamond Bowl.

86. Sapphire Bowl . . . .

The toughest of the bowls to get into, Sapphire requires a tricky bit of navigation through rocks on the edge of a cliff. Traverse right in Garnet Bowl to a bench that splits into an upper and lower traverse line. Take the lower line and sketch your way into the Bowl.

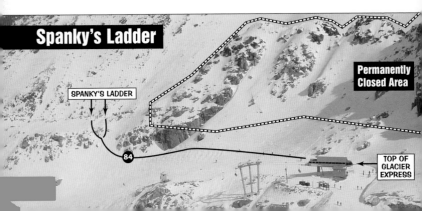

Spanky's Ladder

SPANKY'S LADDER

Permanently Closed Area

84

TOP OF GLACIER EXPRESS

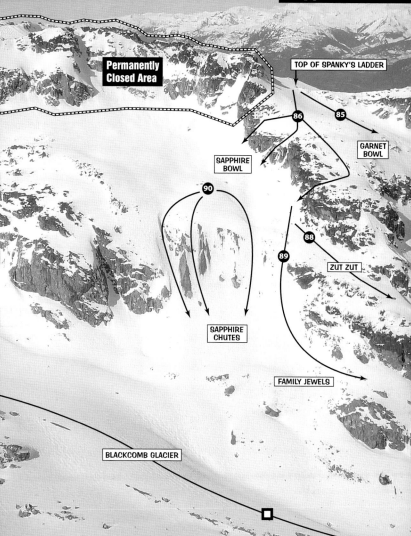

Sapphire Bowl

Permanently Closed Area

TOP OF SPANKY'S LADDER

86

85

GARNET BOWL

SAPPHIRE BOWL

90

88

89

ZUT ZUT

SAPPHIRE CHUTES

FAMILY JEWELS

BLACKCOMB GLACIER

Blackcomb Mountain

 Glacier Express Chair - Diamond Bowl

87. Wild Side . . . .
A way into Diamond Bowl, from the shoulder of Sapphire Bowl.

88. Zut Zut . . . .
A second way to get to Diamond Bowl from Sapphire Bowl, this line forms a fat cornice and snow loads so deeply in here you may need a snorkel!

89. Family Jewels . . . .
The skier's left-most line through Sapphire Bowl eventually traverses left on a bench into Diamond Bowl.

90. Sapphire Chutes . . . .
The upper bowl divides into three chutes that split lower down through old lateral moraines.

91. Diamond Bowl . . . .
Diamond has three entrances from Garnet: Diamond Roll, Diamond Center, and Diamond Left.

92. Calvin . . . .
Enter via Diamond Left and hook left after the diagonal ramp to the slope below the big cliff. Look up and wonder what the guy who tried to jump into this slope from above was thinking!

93. Hobbes . . . .
Directly below Calvin are some short chutes divided by rock bluffs. Hobbes offers many variations, all of which are good.

94. Bad Attitude . . . .
BA is accessed by a traverse left from Calvin through some exposed terrain. Once you are there, you can choose BA proper and trend right or enter the tight gully known as the Roll.

95. Mid-Bowl Roll / Mid-Bowl Gully . . . .
In the centre of Diamond Bowl choose between Mid-Bowl Roll (right) and Mid-Bowl Gully (left).

Diamond Bowl

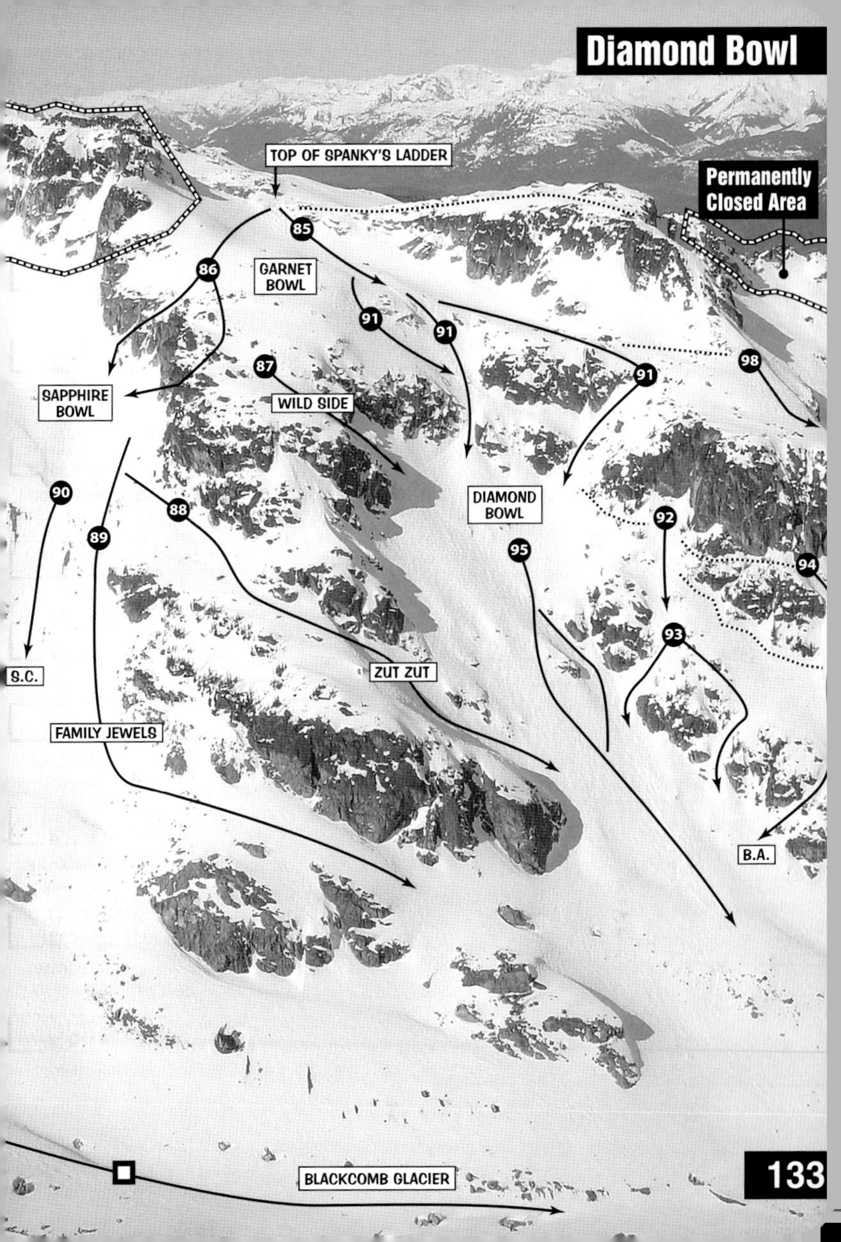
Permanently Closed Area
TOP OF SPANKY'S LADDER
85
86
GARNET BOWL
91
91
91
98
87
SAPPHIRE BOWL
WILD SIDE
90
DIAMOND BOWL
88
92
89
95
94
93
S.C.
ZUT ZUT
FAMILY JEWELS
B.A.
BLACKCOMB GLACIER

Glacier Express Chair - Ruby Bowl

This massive expanse of terrain has two main entrances: Spanky's Chute and Spanky's Shoulder, both of which get you into the complex Ruby Bowl and all its great micro terrain.

96. Spanky's Chute . . . .

From the top of Spanky's Ladder, stay on the ridge and traverse left along the fence until you can slide into the steep chute. Several variations are possible to get into the bowl.

97. Gummy Bear . . . .

A great pocket snowfield accessed high via Spanky's Chute or low via Spanky's Shoulder.

98. Spanky's Shoulder . . . .

From the top of Spanky's Ladder, drop into Garnet Bowl and traverse left below the cliffs. You will arrive at the mellower, convex slope that rolls into Ruby Bowl.

99. Skid Lips . . . .

From the Spanky's Shoulder entrance, drop down the ridge to the edge of the cliff and shred the line on tight skier's right, through the rocks.

100. Playland . . . .

From the bottom of the Skid Lips, tuck right, under the cliff. Traverse skier's right, into the super-fun gully. Enjoy. It is called PLAY Land for a reason!

101. Shredder . . . .

Traverse the upper bowl from Spanky's Chute to the far skier's left. The tight couloir above is called Shredder. Slide in the bottom and rip it until your legs burn.

102. Midway Rock . . . .

Midway refers to the cliff in the upper third of the Bowl. There are two lines, Midway Left and Midway Right. Both are good.

Ruby Bowl

Permanently Closed Area

96

97

98

CLIFF

99

CLIFF

102 CLIFF 102

101

MIDWAY ROCK

SHREDDER

SKID LIPS

100

PLAYLAND

TO BLACKCOMB GLACIER

135

Dan Treadway lights it up on Blackcomb's Ladies First. Photo: Damian Cromwell

Sushilicious

Sachi Sushi 幸

Whistler's Newest Sushi Restaurant

In the Summit Lodge, Main St.

Lunch (call for hours)

Dinner from 5:00

Take-out available

604.935.5649

Best New Restaurant 2003

Best Sushi 2003

Terrain Parks

Whistler Blackcomb is the Mecca of terrain park skiing and riding. Known throughout the industry as the leader in park development and the winner of numerous awards for design and construction, there is something to challenge every level of rider.

The spread of parks and the new breed of talent that has developed is a sure sign of the future of both skiing and snowboarding. If "park" riding is your thing then you have come to the right place. Four parks at Whistler Blackcomb cater to all levels of rider with jumps, boxes, rails, half-pipes and even a wall ride for your jibbing pleasure. The features in terrain parks are all designed for specific intended uses. To reduce your exposure to injury, ensure you are familiar with the proper use of the features or take a lesson.

If you are new to the park riding scene there are some survival tips you need to know. Park users have an unwritten code of conduct that has its roots in both surf line-up and skateboard park etiquette.

- ☐ Ski / Ride features that are appropriate to your ability level. Attempting to ride at a level far beyond your talent makes you a hazard to yourself and others.

- ☐ Before dropping-in to a feature call out that your "Dropping In" to signal your intention to go next.

- ☐ Clear the landing area immediately after you land (or crash if possible).

- ☐ Stop only in a safe place where you are visible to riders above.

- ☐ Dropping in before your turn (snaking) is generally not accepted unless you are by far the best in the park!

1 . . . . 3 T ☐
Chipmunk Bobcat Terrain Park

The Whistler Park. This mid level park has multiple lines offering features for the average rider. The jumps are generally smaller and the pitch less steep than the Blackcomb Parks. This park has grown exponentially over the past few years, gobbling up terrain under the Emerald Express Chair.

2 . . . . 3 HP ☐
Whistler Mountain Nintendo Half-pipe

Whistler Mountain's half-pipe can be found at the top of the Emerald Express Chair. Although small by today's standards it is a great pipe to get the basics dialed. The pipe is groomed and shaped every day by a dedicated group of cat drivers that work exclusively on the parks and pipes.

WHISTLER MOUNTAIN NINTENDO HALF-PIPE

EMERALD EXPRESS CHAIR

CHIPMUNK BOBCAT TERRAIN PARK

3. Big Easy Terrain Garden. . . . .

Located on Blackcomb, below the Last Resort road The Garden offers even the first time park rider a chance to jib. This area has rollers, banks and boxes to get your feet wet. Access the Garden using the Solar Coaster Express chair.

4. Nintendo Terrain Park . . . .

Just below the Solar Coaster Express chair off-load is the "Blackcomb Park" the intermediate spot for getting your park fix. With a massive sound system blasting fresh new vibes from the DJ shack this park offers an array of hips, boxes, rails, banks and jumps.

5. The Highest Level . . . .

Contained within the Nintendo Park is the "HL" park. This is the mother ship of terrain parks where you need a special pass and a helmet just to get in! Even the Birdman (Tony Hawk) was refused entry when he didn't have one!

CHAINSAW RIDGE

CATSKINNER CHAIR

RENDEZVOUS RESTAURANT

NINTENDO
TERRAIN PARK

SOLAR COASTER
EXPRESS CHAIR

HIGHEST LEVEL

NINTENDO
SUPERPIPE

Terrain Parks

. . . . .continued

Go to Guest Relations and they will hook you up with what you need. You'll be throwing "Switch Corked Nines" in no time! This park features the largest most intimidating jumps, rails and movie screen sized wall ride of any park. The "HL" is where the sport is being pushed ever further into the future as the builders think of even more farfetched ideas for new school features. Catskinner is the chair to ride in order to see the action from above.

6. Superpipe . . . .

This monster half-pipe can be found at the bottom of the Nintendo Park on the right side. Groomed nightly with the Zawg, this beast offers a huge 16' transition. If you are serious about pipe riding this is the place for you! The title Superpipe is only given to "Olympic Sized" half-pipes.

7. Boarder Cross . . . .

Also known as the Skier Cross. For the uninitiated a Boarder Cross course is the mountain version of the motor-cross with berms, corners, jumps and whoop-de-do's. In competitions like the X-Games, racers match up four at a time for an all out race to the bottom. Recreationally, the course is fun for showdowns between friends or for cruising alone. Access to the course is through a gate on the right side of the Nintendo Park half way down.

8. Spring / Summer Park . .
. . . .

When May rolls around and Blackcomb shuts down for the season, a new park is built high on Whistler to take advantage of the snow in the Glacier Bowl. The Park is built on the right side of the T-Bar and includes the usual mix of features and a half-pipe when the snow pack allows it.

Wall Ride

. . . .**continued**

When Whistler shuts down in June and Blackcomb opens the Horstman Glacier for summer camps, yet another public park is created. For the diehard park user and the would be pro this is your chance to get a jump on training for the next years competitions and Slope Style events. Hits, rails and a pipe are on the menu every summer, so skip the beach and hit the park!

The Future: . . . .

With the World Cup and Olympic events being held in Whistler in the years ahead you can expect the Park scene to grow even bigger. A new Superpipe has been built above the Base 2 facility on Blackcomb and increased snowmaking capabilities plus the potential for major lighting and sound will make this area the site of night sessions in the not too distant future.

photo: Tim Smith

Instant 16 foot tranny!

Link-Ups & Stuff

The best way to maximize your enjoyment of Whistler / Black-comb is to "link" a few lines together and make an epic long run out of it. Try these.

Whistler Mountain:

From the Peak Chair:

Whistler Bowl ⇒ Surprise

Whistler Bowl ⇒ Shale Slope

Whistler Bowl ⇒ Tiger's Terrace

Whistler Bowl ⇒ Doom and Gloom ⇒ Grand Finale

West Cirque ⇒ Sunrise (or Escalator) ⇒ Grand Finale

West Cirque ⇒ Everglades

West Cirque ⇒ Frog Hollow

From the Harmony Express:

Little Whistler ⇒ Camel Backs ⇒ Back Bowl ⇒ Boot Chutes

Any Harmony Horseshoe ⇒ Boomer Bowl ⇒ Wet Dreams

Blackcomb Mountain

From Showcase T-Bar:

Blowhole ⇨ Surf's Up

Blowhole ⇨ Winky Pop

Ladies First ⇨ Husume Flank

From Spanky's Ladder:

Diamond Left ⇨ Calvin ⇨ Hobbes

Emerald Bowl ⇨ Zut Zut

Spanky's Chute ⇨ Playland

Spanky's Chute ⇨ Shredder

Spanky's Shoulder ⇨ Playland

Blackcomb Bowl:

Couloir Extreme ⇨ Fallers Pillow

Bushrat ⇨ Fallers Pillow

Big Bang ⇨ Blowdown

Quazar ⇨ Staircase

Solar Zone:

Bark Sandwich ⇨ Little Cub

Joe Lammers at ease riding the sluff (left) and Chris Eby airing it out in Lakeside Bowl at Blackcomb (right). Photos: Damian Cromwell

147

Groomed Runs

Whistler Blackcomb has one of the best grooming crews in the ski business! Remember to mix in a few of the classic groomed runs even on those powder days. If you get at them early you may find 10 cm of new snow over smooth soft-pack. Try the following:

Blackcomb Mountain

7th Heaven

- ☐ Cloud Nine (Blue)
- ☐ Panorama (Blue)
- ☐ Southern Comfort (Blue)

Crystal Ridge

- ☐ Ridge Runner (Blue)
- ☐ Twist and Shout (Blue)
- ☐ Rock'n Roll (Blue)

Solar Coaster

- ☐ Honeycomb (Blue)
- ☐ Cruiser (Blue)
- ☐ Gandy Dancer (Blue)

Jersey Cream

- ☐ Jersey Cream (Blue)
- ☐ Cougar Milk (Blue)
- ☐ Zig Zag (Blue)

Whistler Mountain

Emerald / Big Red Express

- ☐ Upper & Lower Franz's (Blue)
- ☐ Upper & Lower Dave Murray Downhill (Blue)
- ☐ Little Red Run (Blue)
- ☐ Ptarmigan (Blue)
- ☐ G.S. (Blue)
- ☐ Bear Paw (Black)

T-Bars

- ☐ T-Bar Run (Blue)
- ☐ Harmony Piste (Blue)

Peak Chair

- ☐ The Saddle (Blue)

The following are must-do tick lists for the rider who has only one day at either Blackcomb Mountain or Whistler Mountain. Either of these lists can be fully ticked in a day if the entire mountain is open. These tours de force will allow views in all directions and give a sample of the best terrain and classic link-ups.

Blackcomb

- ☐ Blowhole ⇢ Surf's Up
- ☐ Ladies First ⇢ Husume Flank
- ☐ Sapphire Bowl ⇢ Zut Zut
- ☐ Wild Side ⇢ Midbowl Gully
- ☐ Spanky's Chute ⇢ Midway Right ⇢ Playland
- ☐ Pakalolo Pillow ⇢ The Bite
- ☐ Secret Bowl ⇢ Dakine
- ☐ Smoked Salmon
- ☐ Couloir Extreme ⇢ Coyote Road ⇢ Baggers ⇢ Bite
- ☐ False Face ⇢ Feather Tree
- ☐ Bushrat ⇢ Faller's Pillow
- ☐ Bushrat Shoulder ⇢ high traverse out at Hot Tub ⇢ Glades off 7th Ave
- ☐ Heart Throb ⇢ Sluiceway (see mountain map)

Whistler

- ☐ Excitation
- ☐ The Couloir
- ☐ Whistler Bowl ⇢ Shale Slope
- ☐ West Cirque ⇢ Sunrise ⇢ Grand Finale
- ☐ Stefan's Chute ⇢ West Bowl
- ☐ Harmony Ridge ⇢ Boomer Bowl ⇢ Wet Dreams
- ☐ Pig's Fancy
- ☐ Little Whistler ⇢ Camel Back ⇢ Boot Chutes
- ☐ McConkey's
- ☐ Sun Bowl ⇢ Crescendo
- ☐ Harmony Ridge ⇢ Harvey's Harrow
- ☐ T-Bar Run ⇢ Old Man ⇢ Franz's ⇢ the valley

About the Authors

Brian Finestone is employed year-round as the Public Safety Supervisor for Whistler and Blackcomb Mountains. He has dedicated over ten years to providing rescue services in the mountains, working in Canada and abroad as a professional ski patroller, avalanche forecaster and avalanche rescue dog handler.

Originally in Whistler for a one-season break from university, Brian quickly realized he would never be content to return to the world of academia. Inspired by an avalanche dog team he met while working as a lift operator in 1992, Brian focused on the hard skills required to work in the field of mountain rescue, eventually becoming a senior avalanche rescue dog handler and president of the Canadian Avalanche Rescue Dog Association.

A self-described "alpine generalist", Brian is equally at home on alpine skis, snowboard, telemark skis or with a pair of ice axes in hand. His passion for winter mountain sports can only be eclipsed by his passion for rock climbing in any of its different forms. Brian

Acknowledgments

Just like at the Academy Awards, writing a book gives you the platform and podium to thank all the people behind the scenes who helped make your dreams a reality. So here goes…

We would like to thank the following:

Marc Bourdon for inspiration, guidance and helping us create a product of exceptional quality. Ian Hodder for editing volumes of our grammatically incorrect sentences. Nigel Stewart and Joe Lammers for their careful proofreading. Scott Flavelle for his aerial lens work. Tim Smith and Joe Hertz for access to their well-documented archive of photography. Naomi Jaremczuk for graphic design work done "in a pinch". Alain Denis, Bryn Hughes and Damian Cromwell for their awesome images and

resides in Whistler with his wife Abbie, young son Finn and a new puppy destined for a career in avalanche rescue.

photo on left: Bonny Makarewicz, photo on right: Brian Finestone

Kevin Hodder splits his time between guiding in the mountains and working as a television producer. He is certified by the Association of Canadian Mountain Guides as a Rock-Climbing Guide, Assistant Alpine-Climbing Guide and Assistant Ski Guide.

Kevin has long served as the Race Manager for the Eco-Challenge expedition race, which has taken him to such locales as Australia, Morocco, Argentina, Malaysia, New Zealand and Fiji. His work can also be seen on the popular television series "Survivor" (CBS) where he is a member of the team responsible for designing and coordinating the challenges. At the time of publication he was working on the much-publicized show "The Contender" (NBC).

Kevin has climbed and skied at several international locations and maintains a boyish enthusiasm for both. To facilitate his schedule he resides with his girlfriend, Meredith, in both Whistler and Santa Monica, California.

their dedication to showcasing local athletes. Whistler Blackcomb and its Senior Leadership Team for endorsing our idea and supporting the project. Brian Leighton and Robert Kennedy for their invaluable advice and words of encouragement.

A final thanks goes to our families, Abbie and Finn Finestone and Meredith Rozbitsky for tolerating our manic and depressive personalities as the project developed. And, of course, our parents for buying us our first pairs of skis in the third grade.

You have all made a large impact on this book and we sincerely appreciate it!

Glossary

Advanced:
A term used to describe someone capable of skiing or snowboarding black diamond terrain.

Alpine:
A term used to describe the portion of the mountain above the "tree line".

Avalanche:
Massive amounts of snow sliding down hill gathering momentum and force as it travels.

Backcountry:
The fabled land beyond the boundary ropes where the only rules are the laws of nature.

Beginner:
A skier or snowboarder learning to master the skills required to successfully slide down a Green run without falling.

Big Dump:
A large amount of snow accumulated from a single storm.

Booter:
Slang for a large jump, typically found in the terrain park, or built by visitors in the backcountry.

Bootpack:
A place where people walk up hill to access certain runs. A track is often formed by people packing the snow down with their boots.

Bowl:
A dish shaped alpine feature that is famous for catching and preserving powder.

Cat Track:
A ski run, the width of a single lane road. Cat tracks are used by snowcats, snowmobiles and skiers alike.

Chute:
A narrow ribbon of snow between ridges of rock. The width of a chute can range from several meters to less than a ski length. It is synonymous with the French word "Couloir"

Couloir:
French for "hall way". It is synonymous with "chute".

Cruiser:
A well-groomed slope with wide-open space for high speed, large radius turns.

Cruising:
Carving wide turns on flat well-groomed slopes, typically at moderate to high rates of speed.

Downloading:
Riding a chairlift down the mountain instead of skiing. Downloading is often used for mountain egress early or late in the season when valley snow is nonexistent.

Expert:
A term used to describe skiers and snowboarders capable of descending double black diamond terrain…and make it look easy!

Fall Line:
The line a snowball would take if you rolled it downhill. Expert skiers are always looking for the fall line.

Fat Conditions:
Slang for deep snow in a seasonal accumulation context or when referring to a significant snowfall from a storm.

Gate:
The skiing equivalent of the "velvet rope". A gate is simply a break in the fence line that is opened and closed at the discretion of the ski patrol.

Glades:
Refers to areas with widely spaced trees. Glades are sought after terrain because the quality of the snow can be preserved by the trees yet they are wide enough to easily turn around.

Hip Jump:
An embankment jump encountered in the terrain park where riders ride up the take off ramp and re-enter at 90 degrees on another transition.

Huckster:
A snow enthusiast with a penchant for hurling themselves off precipices. The huckster will often jump over objects rather than slide around them.

Intermediate:
A skier or snowboarder that is capable of turning both ways and stopping. The intermediate is now able to venture into increasingly difficult terrain but may struggle in powder.

Lightboard:
A billboard which, through the illumination of specific lights, indicates which lifts are opened, closed and on standby. It may also detail how long the lines are at each lift. Lightboards are placed conveniently on both mountains.

Magic Carpet:
A conveyer belt used to transport beginner skiers up hill. An evolutionary leap from the dreaded rope tow.

Mogul:
A hardened lump of snow created by constant traffic over a slope that elicits dread or joy depending on the state of your knees and back.

Moraine:
A large row of rock formed by the movement of glacial ice.

Park Rider:
A breed of snowboarder found almost exclusively in the terrain park with exceptional skill and a thick file at the medical clinic.

Park Skier:
A breed of skier also found in the terrain park, recognizable by the unique clothing style and ability to ski equally well forward or backward.

Pitch:
Two meanings: 1/ the angle or steepness of a slope. 2/ The length of slope one can ski before reaching the bottom or stopping to rest.

Playstation:
A digital distraction to the world of reality, referred to as a "Not-getting-paid-Station" by those who are unemployed.

Poaching:
Riding a closed run. Don't do it.

Powder:
Often referred to as "White Gold", powder is snow with a very low specific gravity and a tendency to make people sick for work.

Puking:
Slang term for a particularly hard snowfall, eliciting feelings of excitement when occurring the night before a day on the mountain.

Pungy Tree:
Small treetops or branches buried just below or protruding from the snow surface. May create a tripping hazard to unsuspecting skiers and riders.

Rider / Snowboarder:
The saviors of the ski industry, loved by some hated by others, but here to stay.

Glossary

Schralp:
Slang term for the tracking up of powder snow, refers to the laying down of tracks until all the virgin snow is gone.

Shred:
Slang term, similar to schralp, describing the act of snowboarding an untracked area. The word was coined by the snowboard movement in the early eighties.

Sideslipping:
This action involves sliding down a run with your edges perpendicular to the fall line. The result is often the formation of an ugly groove and the scraping of soft surface snow off the run.

Skier:
A broad term used to describe any one on two planks (lengths may vary) who slides down the mountain; variations include telemark, snowblades and fat skis with an eclectic mix of human participants of all shapes and sizes.

Skier's Left:
The left-hand side of the ski run from the perspective of a skier sliding down the fall line.

Skier's Right:
The right-hand side of the slope from the perspective of a skier sliding down the fall line.

Sluff:
A small avalanche of snow that is released as a rider carves turns. Warning; a sluff can develop into an avalanche if enough snow becomes entrained.

Snowcat:
Large machines on metal tracks, capable of grooming runs and plowing snow.

Sweep:
A term used to describe the patrol clearing of the mountain. From top to bottom the entire mountain is skied to ensure no public are left on-hill after closing.

Thigh Burner:
A long run requiring stamina in the quadriceps femora muscles, the term is relative, so one persons thigh burner may be another person's warm up run.

Tranny:
Park slang for transition. The ramp portion of a jump or half-pipe's take off and landing.

Treeline:
A term used in avalanche forecasting to describe the elevation where trees begin to grow, also referred to as the "subalpine" in ski literature.

Tree Well:
A tree well is a dangerous natural phenomenon where a hole forms around the base of a tree. (See safety section)

Index of Advertisers

The following companies and retailers have been very generous in supporting this project. Knee Deep Productions and Quickdraw Publications would like to thank the following:

Index

Index

Scott Gaffney takes the big drop. Photo: Bryn Hughes